ALCTS Papers on Library Technical Services and Collections, #17

# RISK AND
# ENTREPRENEURSHIP IN LIBRARIES
## Seizing Opportunities for Change

Pamela Bluh and Cindy Hepfer,
editors

Association for Library Collections
& Technical Services
American Library Association

CHICAGO   2009

# ALCTS PAPERS ON LIBRARY TECHNICAL SERVICES AND COLLECTIONS SERIES

*Future of the Descriptive Cataloging Rules, #6*

    Edited by Brian E. C. Schottlaender, 135p. 1996, ALA Editions.
ISBN: 0-8389-3477-3

*Collection Management and Development: Issues in an Electronic Era, #5*

    Edited by Peggy Johnson and Bonnie MacEwan, 148p. 1993,
ALA Editions. ISBN: 0-8389-3447-1

*Format Integration and Its Effect on Cataloging, Training, and Systems, #4*

    Edited by Karen Coyle, 100p. 1993, ALA Editions.
ISBN: 0-8389-3432-3

*Collection Management for the 1990s, #3*

    Edited by Joseph J. Branin, 178p. 1992, ALA Editions.
ISBN: 0-8389-0608-7

*Origins, Content, and Future of AACR2 Revised, #2*

    Edited by Richard P. Smiraglia, 139p. 1992, ALA Editions.
ISBN: 0-8389-3405-6

*Subject Authorities in the Online Environment, #1*

    Edited by Karen Markey, 84p. 1991, ALA Editions.
ISBN: 0-8389-0558-7

Association for Library Collections & Technical Services (ALCTS)
ALCTS is a division of the American Library Association

Proceeds from ALCTS professional publications help support the programs and other member services of ALCTS.

ALCTS Publishing
50 E. Huron St.
Chicago, IL 60611
www.ala.org/alcts

**Library of Congress Cataloging-in-Publication Data**

    Risk and entrepreneurship in libraries : seizing opportunities for change /
        Pamela Bluh and Cindy Hepfer, editors.p. cm.—(ALCTS papers on library
        technical services & collections ; #17)
    Includes bibliographical references.
    ISBN 978-0-8389-8516-8
    1. Library administration. 2. Organizational change. 3. Entrepreneurship.
        I. Bluh, Pamela. II. Hepfer, Cindy.
    Z678.R54 2009025.1—dc222009020289

ISBN: 978-0-8389-8516-8

Published in the United States of America.

# Contents

# Introduction

PAMELA BLUH and CINDY HEPFER

> It is common sense to take a method and try it. If it fails, admit
> it frankly and try another. But above all, try something.
> —*Franklin D. Roosevelt*

The universal nature of those words, written in 1933 by Franklin Delano Roosevelt, inspired and motivated a country and a people during the height of the Great Depression. They seem as appropriate in 2009 as they were then and entirely fitting as the inspiration for a book dealing with risk and entrepreneurship.

In stereotypical fashion, librarians are often described as old fuddy-duddies, stuck in a rut, and too timid to experiment with new ways of doing things. In 2007, before chinks in the national (and global) economic and sociopolitical façade became visible, librarians were already aware that the library landscape had changed. It was with that knowledge that the idea for a symposium to explore the topic of risk and showcase entrepreneurial activities in libraries was conceived by members of the 2008 ALCTS President's Program Committee. In January 2008, in Philadelphia, ALCTS presented the Midwinter Symposium *Risk and Entrepreneurship in Libraries: Seizing Opportunities for Change.*

Transformative actions are urgently needed if libraries and the practice of librarianship are to flourish. The contributors to this book represent a variety of backgrounds and points of view, yet their examination

---

Introductory quote from Franklin D. Roosevelt, *Looking Forward* (New York: John Day, 1933), 51.

of the way libraries manage risk and their perspectives on entrepreneurial enterprises appear to be quite similar. They recognize that maintaining the status quo is not possible and that to play a dominant role in the lives of their communities, librarians need to take risks and seize entrepreneurial opportunities.

Marshall Keys, the well-known consultant, self-confessed *flaneur* (someone who strolls around in apparent idleness observing the world) and entrepreneur sets the tone for the publication (as he did when he gave the opening address at the symposium) with an essay entitled *Entrepreneurship and Risk in Libraries: Seizing and Creating Opportunities for Change.* Keys characterizes himself as someone whose passion is "helping libraries prepare for change, especially the kinds of changes that technology [brings]."[1] Using behavioral economics as a framework, Keys examines the process of change from a practical point of view, conveying his familiarity with risk and entrepreneurship in the not-for-profit sector and offering useful strategies for managing risk.

Conversations about risk and entrepreneurship in libraries must take into account questions about copyright and intellectual property. Professor Michael Carroll, an expert on intellectual property and cyberlaw, is well-positioned to assess the risks and opportunities associated with acquiring, managing, digitizing, and providing access to collections. Carroll is a member of the Board of Directors of the Creative Commons, Inc. and a staunch advocate for open access to scholarly literature. In *Copyright, Fair Use, and Creative Commons Licenses,* he explains what is meant by the "public domain," discusses the fundamentals of fair use, and describes the advantages of acquiring materials under a Creative Commons license.

In *Moderately Risky Business: Challenging Librarians to Assume More Risk in an Era of Opportunity,* Joyce Ogburn points out the delicate balance that exists between risk and entrepreneurship. She describes a number of interesting challenges for libraries and explains how these challenges offer both risks and opportunities. Librarians must learn to manage risk so that they can navigate successfully through a changing universe and create an environment which is, first and foremost, responsive to the needs of library users. Ogburn makes a strong argument for the value of experimentation coupled with an understanding and appreciation of the underlying risks.

For a subject that is often underappreciated and difficult to understand, Regina Reynolds and Diane Boehr provide a fascinating and clear approach to the business of cataloging in *Bibliographic Control 2.0? Entrepreneurial Lessons from Web 2.0.* They outline both the risks of a business-as-usual approach to cataloging as well as the potential rewards of employing new strategies for access and discovery. Reynolds and Boehr discuss the importance of several of the recommendations in the report of the LC Working Group on the Future of Bibliographic Control and the urgency of making library processes Web 2.0-enabled.

Providing a counterbalance to the papers that offer a global approach to risk and entrepreneurship are chapters by Amy Badertscher and Lynne Scott Cochrane, as well as Jeff Trzeciak. Both these chapters describe risks they and their libraries took to establish a climate conducive to change. *Two College Libraries Merge Their Technical Services Departments: A Case Study of Denison University and Kenyon College* by Cochrane and Badertscher outlines the painstaking research and study that ultimately led to the ground-breaking merger of the two technical services departments. Jeff Trzeciak's *McMaster University Libraries 2.0: Transforming Traditional Organizations* provides an overview of the transformation of the McMaster University Library from a tradition-bound academic library into "an innovative, user-centered partner" within the university. Trzeciak displays a flare for the dramatic and clearly grabs the reader's attention with his passionate description of the changes that have already taken place, as well as those still being planned, at McMaster.

Taking a more provocative approach to the topic, public librarian Rivkah Sass believes that her peers must develop a much stiffer backbone and be much less risk-averse if they are going to create friendlier, more efficient environments for their users. The title, *Warning: When Rowing Forward This Boat May Rock!*, recalls an ancient Chinese proverb and serves as a reminder that even with the most careful planning and taking into account all eventualities, there may be strong opposition to change.

In the September/October 2008 issue of *Technicalities*, Diane Hillman wrote, "sometimes being embedded in traditional practice can blind us to the possibilities of new approaches."[2] Now more than ever, as they face threats to their continued relevance, librarians should take this observation to heart. As Rivkah Sass noted, "instead of seeing themselves and their institutions as unique, [it is time for] librarians in all types of libraries to consider what their organizations have in common and build on that commonality."[3] The authors represented in this book have skillfully illustrated how ambitious, energetic librarians can transform their organizations, re-envision library services, and focus attention on the needs of library users. By managing risk, by doing due diligence, by sharing their experiences, by supporting each other, and by encouraging entrepreneurial enterprises, librarians will be well positioned to seize and create opportunities.

## REFERENCE NOTES

1. "Snapshot: Marshall Keys," *Information Link* 8, no. 2 (February 2004): 2, http://my.simmons.edu/gslis/docs/il/03-04/Information_Link_2-04.pdf (accessed 20 April 2009).

2. Diane Hillman, "Talk to Me about Terminology Services!" *Technicalities* 28, no. 5 (Sept./Oct. 2008): 7.

3. Rivkah Sass, "Warning: When Rowing Forward This Boat May Rock!" *Risk and Entrepreneurship in Libraries: Seizing Opportunities for Change,* Pamela Bluh and Cindy Hepfer, eds. (Chicago: ALA/ALCTS, 2009), 103.

# Entrepreneurship and Risk in Libraries

## *Seizing and Creating Opportunities for Change*

MARSHALL KEYS

Writing about entrepreneurship and risk in the fall of 2008 is very different than writing in the fall of 2007 when this article was conceived. Our country, indeed the world, has seen the consequences of unanticipated and uncontrolled risk to our economy and society, and we have watched these changes lead to global crisis and confusion.

And yet as I write in mid-November 2008, it is becoming clear that a widespread failure to take any risk at all is very likely to prove at least as destructive as the initial collapse of the housing and securities markets. Failing to take risk is a failure of trust, which leads to economic deflation, the condition where the value of assets falls because no one trusts the future enough to buy or hold them at a price that rewards the sellers for the risk they take in developing the assets.

A bank lacks faith that a retailer can sell televisions, so the bank refuses a loan to buy new televisions. Buyers come into the store and don't find merchandise to buy, even when they have the money. Manufacturers lack outlets for their goods, so they dump them at extremely low prices in places that can purchase them for cash. The original retailer can't make a sale that recovers the price he paid, and the whole process spirals downward again.

Libraries are not immune to this cycle. When libraries don't take on risk, the collection suffers (e.g., users complain that there's never any new stuff) and services fail to keep pace with developments in the wider world. The result is deflation in the perceived value of libraries in the eye of the consumer, leading to a loss of political and financial support, and our own downward spiral. Accepting risk is a necessary condition for progress.

Entrepreneurs are people who accept risk. Mountain climbers distinguish between two kinds of risk: objective risk, which is out of their control; and subjective risk, which can be controlled by planning, preparing, and prudence. A library that loses external funding suffers from an objective risk. A library that fails to manage its resources experiences the consequences of a subjective risk.

The following look at entrepreneurship, managing risk, and creating organizational change is based on an operational framework of experience. This is written from (what I hope is) an entirely practical point of view, built on a theoretical framework of behavioral economics. My mission is helping readers understand how people behave under stress and what can be done about it. People are one of the risks over which one has some control.

Topics include:

- General introduction to entrepreneurship;
- Entrepreneurship in existing organizations, especially in not-for-profits;
- What aspiring entrepreneurs ought to do and what they ought not to do;
- What entrepreneurs can expect to go wrong and why;
- What they can do about going wrong;
- The biggest risks and how to manage them.

## ENTREPRENEURSHIP

An entrepreneur is a person who creates value through innovation. Innovation is the entrepreneur's response to change in the environment. Most people see change as threatening. Entrepreneurs see opportunity in new situations, and most of them are happiest in turbulence. Entrepreneurial innovation is vision-driven; most people focus on the present and are generally satisfied. Entrepreneurs look at the existing situation and have a vision of where the world should be tomorrow. Without change, there is no entrepreneurship.

An intrapreneur is a person within a large organization who takes direct responsibility for turning an idea into a finished product through assertive risk-taking and innovation (from [intra(corporate) + (ENTRE)PRENEUR]).[1] The key characteristics are assertiveness, risk-taking, and innovation.

## Adding Value

Successful entrepreneurship adds value. Innovation that does not add value is unsustainable. The value added through innovation may be monetary, and indeed, that is what we usually think of when we look at the motivation of entrepreneurs: they want to get rich. Entrepreneurs can add value by developing new businesses and new sources of revenue or by lowering costs. Both approaches add monetary value.

The value added can also be intangible. An entrepreneur can focus on increasing quality or enhancing customer satisfaction, both of which add value outside the organization, and at the same time enhance its prestige or reputation. An entrepreneur can also focus on internal issues such as improving the work environment and giving employees a greater sense of accomplishment in what they do. The ideal entrepreneur will do all of these. Steve Jobs and Bill Gates are entrepreneurs who have created value both within and outside their organizations. Customers buy their products and people want to work for Apple and Microsoft and feel good about doing it.

Entrepreneurs characteristically add value by:

- developing new products and programs;
- reengineering processes;
- cutting organizations loose from unsuccessful products and programs.

All of these actions involve uncertainty, which is felt as risk. All change involves risk. Any time we do something new, failure is a possible result.

Entrepreneurs often fail, but unlike most of us, they accept failure, learn the appropriate lessons, and move on. Because they are vision-driven, entrepreneurs are not destroyed by failure. Entrepreneurs usually believe the vision was right even if the environment, the timing, and the execution were not. Since all these are sources of risk, successful entrepreneurs must learn to assess and manage risk. Either by training or experience, they must learn to observe the environment realistically, choose the time for their action carefully, and be obsessive about execution.

## The Entrepreneur in the World

In the popular mind, the entrepreneur is usually a loner. Think of carmaker Preston Tucker or Howard Roark in Ayn Rand's *The Fountainhead*. In reality, entrepreneurs cannot be loners. Entrepreneurs cannot achieve their vision by themselves. They must achieve their vision through others—a team. This introduces what is a critical moral issue for entrepreneurs: how do entrepreneurs innovate *with* others rather than *over* others?

This matters because there is a thin line between vision and monomania. There are entrepreneurs who will exhaust all the resources they can get—their own and those belonging to other people—alienate their friends, spouses, and children, and make life miserable for their associates, all in pursuit of a vision. How can entrepreneurs make sure that their entrepreneurship remains in balance with their ethics and their relationships? How can entrepreneurs be sure that the scarce resources they use—and resources are almost always scarce—are best used in the pursuit of their vision? What if they are wrong? What if their vision is wrong?

Finally, because entrepreneurship demands a great deal of commitment and because it may create serious consequences in other people's lives, how do entrepreneurs assure that they are not simply creating change for the sake of change? Cartoon character Dilbert's boss once moved around everyone in the office so "my people" will form a square. We have all worked for people like that. We just don't want to *be* people like that.

## ENTREPRENEURSHIP IN ORGANIZATIONS

Entrepreneurship in existing organizations is much more difficult than starting from scratch. There are established structures and infrastructures to get around and plenty of oxen waiting to be gored. But the most difficult issue is trying to look outside the box when one is living in the box. Many people believe that the global investment bank Lehman Brothers went bankrupt in the summer of 2008 because the CEO had been with the firm for forty-two years. He just couldn't imagine the firm being any different than it had always been. The CEOs of General Motors, Ford, and Chrysler appeared on Capitol Hill in November 2008 to beg for cash to prevent the imminent collapse of their companies, but all came individually in corporate jets. The concept of an impending collapse should have moved the CEOs to look for cost-cutting measures, including their own transportation to Washington. This thoughtlessness outraged Congress, the press, and the American public. Established patterns are difficult to escape, and when people manage to break the patterns they often fall prey to analysis paralysis: becoming so focused on the "what ifs" and indecision that nothing happens until it is too late.

Financial management and advisory company Merrill Lynch survived by being acquired. Its CEO was so new that he was able to think of a potential collapse as an abstract business problem. He recognized that his job was to salvage the company and its employees and investors, not to preserve it as it was. This is why businesses, universities, and libraries so often hire outsiders as change agents. But anyone can ask what kind of change is needed: revision or just reprocess? Changing work itself or just how it's done?

Those who work in libraries rarely have the option of starting a new library when a better way of doing things presents itself. Except in periods of very rapid technological change—for example during the early days of the development of local systems—we cannot go to venture capitalists and seek funding for a whole new way of doing things. We are stuck in organizations and with funding from existing resources and must carry out change mostly with existing staff and resources.

## Entrepreneurship in Not-for-Profits

Entrepreneurial personalities will not be happy in traditional organizations. Traditional not-for-profit organizations are characteristically hierarchies, centrally controlled, with staff focused on specialized duties and directed by rules and statutes. This is the typical library.

Entrepreneurial not-for-profits are mission-focused, decentralized, and team-oriented, though with integrated responsibilities.

In traditional not-for-profits, employees are accountable for following rules, focusing on what is best for the organization, emphasizing working within programs, and defining quality by professional standards as in, for example, "The Endoscopy Clinic at Brigham and Women's Hospital accredited by the AAAASF" or "ALA-accredited degree required."[2]

Employees in entrepreneurial organizations are accountable for outcomes, not for following rules. They focus on what is best for the client, not what is easiest for the organization. Quality is defined by meeting customer needs and expectations.

Traditional not-for-profits are monopolies, generally dependent on external funding. Thus they are focused on controlling costs and on trying to satisfy as large a group as possible by being all things to all people.

Entrepreneurial not-for-profits are generally self-supporting and recognize that clients have multiple options. They are focused on providing value, usually to a selected group of clients. They are usually focused on niche rather than universal services.

The entrepreneur's job in a not-for-profit is to move the organization from traditional toward entrepreneurial habits of thought and modes of action. Many large organizations can never become truly entrepreneurial because of external financial and governance constraints, but programs within these organizations can be developed and managed as entrepreneurial—intrapreneurial, if you will—initiatives.

## HOW TO BE A SUCCESSFUL ENTREPRENEUR

Suppose you have a vision of a different future, a different way of providing services, and different way of doing things. Suppose you have support in implementing that vision from those you work for.

### What Do You Do?

#### COMMUNICATE YOUR VISION

Share the vision with everyone who will be involved in implementing it, and you must change their vision to reflect yours. You must gain agreement that this is where the organization is and that is where it must be. This is enormously difficult to do across an organization, and much of what follows deals with those difficulties.

In order to change the focus of the organization, you have to have and communicate a clear idea of what you want to do. What is the present state? What is the future state (vision)? What is the innovation, the value proposition, that gets you from now to then?

Can you explain all this in a sentence?

Perhaps not, but one structured way to communicate a vision is a business plan. Business plans can and should have numeric components, but before collecting and focusing on numbers, the entrepreneur needs to answer the following questions:

- What are we going to do?
- What value will it add? (How will it make things better?)
- What resources will be required?
- How will those resources be obtained?
- How will the work be organized?
- How will the results be marketed?
- How will the project be evaluated?
- How will we know when to kill it off, for all good things come to an end?

Successful entrepreneurs communicate. They share information and expect others to share as well. They share bad news as well as good, they share up and down the organization, not just in the executive suite or in-group, and, most important, they listen to what they get back. No one should feel that his views of the vision have gone unheard, and no employee should ever see a business or program collapse without knowing it was in trouble. This is what happened at Lehman Brothers and American energy giant Enron Corporation before they collapsed, and it is just plain unethical for leaders to put people in that position.

## GAIN TRUST

It is not enough to communicate. The second thing the entrepreneur must do to gain the trust and cooperation of others is to embody the entrepreneurial behavior to be evoked. Much of the great anger at business leaders in the U.S. in the fall of 2008 has come from their own excessive behavior and their unwillingness to accept the consequences of that behavior. They are rightly criticized for wanting it both ways, "capitalism on the way up, and socialism on the way down." This critical economic concept is called "moral hazard." It requires those who profit from taking risks to accept responsibility for a loss when that is the consequence of their action. Responsible entrepreneurs must walk the walk as well as talk the talk.

Thus the entrepreneur must accept the necessity of risk and when necessary put her career on the line by repeating the entrepreneur's mantra: "It is easier to ask forgiveness than to ask permission." If one believes in something, one should do it but be prepared to accept the consequences if failure results. At the same time, an entrepreneurial leader will create an environment that is safe for innovation by reducing the cost of failure for others.

## CLEARLY DEFINE ISSUES

The third and most difficult task for the entrepreneur is defining the issues clearly. Problems that have not been defined correctly cannot be solved, and most people simply do not think clearly. They work with inaccurate information, they use inconsistent logic, they accept all kinds of illusions, and they make use of all sorts of mental shortcuts. The latter part of this paper will discuss this in more detail, but here are four common examples of impaired thinking.

> *Believing what we want to believe rather than facts.* In 2004, most people in the academic world assumed that John Kerry was more intelligent than George W. Bush. The facts however show that they went to equally rigorous prep schools, but Bush had marginally better grades at Yale, marginally better scores on the military General Classification Test, and went to a better graduate school than

Kerry. George Bush had many problems, but they weren't based on being less intelligent than John Kerry.[3]

*Thinking inconsistently.* Television evangelist Joyce Meyer cautions young viewers, "Avoid sex out of wedlock! STD viruses are constantly mutating and growing more deadly!" Does Meyer believe in evolution? No, she is inconsistent.

*Thinking with illusions.* Men and women are different. Cartoons in the *New Yorker* make this point all the time. Women managers are frequently frustrated that managing men is different from managing women, and Henry Higgins' question in the musical *My Fair Lady*, "Why Can't a Woman be More like a Man?" continues to plague male managers. One gender is not better than the other; it is just different, and we forget this at our peril.

*Using mental shortcuts.* If someone tells you that Kevin enjoys chess, goes to classical music concerts, and takes dates to museums, is he more likely to be a salesman or a librarian? Most people would answer "librarian" because these kinds of activities are often associated with librarians of both genders. But the answer is likely to be wrong because it ignores the *base rate*. There are so many more male salesmen than male librarians that for any given set of interests or characteristics, there are likely to be more salesmen in the pool. We all plan from too few data points: "everyone I know thinks . . .", "my users don't want . . . ."

## TAKE CARE OF THE SMALL STUFF

Finally, the successful entrepreneur needs to be prepared to do a lot of essentially boring work. Life is not all raising the flag on the barricades. Successful entrepreneurs reduce risk by sweating the details, including reading everything that comes across their desks.

Many business documents are boring and most of us lack the formal training to assess them appropriately. It is easy to assume that someone else will catch problems or that we can trust our vendor to act on our behalf. The town of Narvik, Norway, suffered heavy losses when pension fund investments linked to the American subprime mortgage market soured. The leaders of the municipality did not read the prospectus before voting to authorize the investment because they trusted Terra Securities, with which the town had worked since the late 1990s.[4]

In the U.S., the collapse of Rowecom left many libraries in the lurch, in some cases with losses of up to $500,000. Librarians had dealt with Rowecom and its predecessor for years, and they expected Rowecom to be around forever, yet the company had failed before and all the evidence of impending collapse was in its SEC reports. Librarians trusted the company.

Reading the fine print is part of understanding that ultimately you are responsible for everything. You can delegate the work, but you cannot delegate the responsibility. If there are things you don't understand in a contract or proposal, get someone else to explain it to you—another staff member, someone in the accounting department, or a lawyer. If an idea sounds too good to be true, it is. As an entrepreneur, one really can't afford to take anything on trust. People who will micromanage staff to death will blithely sign commitments that they haven't read. Trust no one—but not in a paranoid way.

## What Not to Do

Entrepreneurs do things that almost guarantee problems in a project, most of them arising from the very enthusiasm that leads the entrepreneur into a project in the first place. Entrepreneurs must always guard against anything that could be perceived as a display of ego.

### ANNOUNCE PROJECTS IMMEDIATELY

*Wait until the effort is working and successful.* This creates a safe climate for innovation by lowering the risk of failure. Never announce a project until it has been in successful beta for at least six months. Scientists seldom announce their laboratory failures, and Edison is reported to have said, "I have not failed. I have successfully discovered 1,200 ideas that don't work." Unsuccessful projects will fade away if they are not hyped to begin with. The key issue is: what has been learned from the project?

### GET EMOTIONAL

*Powerful people don't yell.* One of the things that Marlon Brando understood in his brilliant portrayal of Don Vito Corleone in *The Godfather* was that not raising his voice was a sign of his power. Other people had to work to hear him; he never raised his voice to accommodate others. Former Harvard President Laurence Summers is famous for being abrasive. He was not named Secretary of the Treasury in the Obama administration despite being the most brilliant economist of his generation. Many commentators saw a connection between this and his abrasiveness.

## TAKE ALL THE CREDIT

*Don't just show up for the photo.* Give all the credit for success to other people. They will appreciate it, and those who matter will know who deserves the credit. You have the responsibility for failure; you will get the credit for success.

## BLAME EVERYONE, INCLUDING YOURSELF

*Don't blame others.* If a project does not succeed it is not because the wrong people were chosen, or because it was envisioned poorly, or because insufficient resources were provided. It is not the fault of the people involved. People fail. Get over it. Don't blame yourself, either. Learn not to make the same mistake again.

## WHAT'S GOING TO GO WRONG AND WHY

Things generally go wrong for three reasons, sometimes singly and sometimes in combination.

### Dysfunctional Systems

This is often the case in very large organizations where competing interests impair the effectiveness of the whole. Systems are set up to be safe, not to be transforming or even efficient. For years, purchasing agents have said "No one ever got fired for buying IBM." The whole purpose of unions is to reduce risk and increase the perceived safety of their members, yet again and again, unions haven't been able to protect workers when there was a radical change in the environment.

The bidding system for purchasing local systems in libraries is deeply flawed. It poisons the relationship between customer and vendor because it is a closed auction. What's "up for bid" is the library's money. Vendors bid services to win that money and libraries encourage them to bid lots of services. Because it is a closed auction, vendors don't know what other vendors are bidding and vendors always bid (promise) more than they can realistically deliver.[5]

In most closed auctions, successful bidders generally bid twice what they should. In the library system business, vendors can't deliver what they promise and still make a profit, so they slow development and delivery, and the library is an unhappy customer. Neither side is bad, neither side is incompetent. The system is flawed.

Richard Thaler, who helped publicize this problem, is a behavioral economist. Behavioral economics has its origin in the work of two Israeli-born psychologists, Daniel Kahneman and Amos Tversky, who studied how people made choices. The best known behavioral economist is probably Steve Leavitt, whose book *Freakonomics* first brought the discipline to popular attention.[6]

## Human Risk

Behavioral economics offers a way of reducing the human risk in organizations by understanding how people make decisions. That matters because the second major reason that entrepreneurial projects fail is that people make mistakes, they just plain screw up. The good news is that people behave irrationally and screw up in certain well-defined and identifiable ways. Behavioral economics attempts to define, describe, and suggest techniques to manage the limits on rational behavior that lead to bad decisions. It is a useful technique because it takes the bad guy-good guy concept out of discussions. We are all limited in some ways and once we learn the patterns, we can recognize irrational behavior—our own and others'!

The last point is important because the third most common reason for failure is that the entrepreneur screws up.

## Stress and Cognitive Errors

Psychologists Amos Tversky and Daniel Kahneman have shown that when people are confronted with uncertainty, they are more likely to make cognitive errors.[7]

As entrepreneurs create necessary changes, they also create a great deal of uncertainty, which can lead to emotional stress for participants and can also lead to cognitive errors described and confirmed by the research of Tversky and Kahneman. Research has shown again and again that people who resist change overvalue what they have and undervalue the alternatives. This is called the Endowment Effect, which reflects the belief that whatever the individual has is better than anything that can be expected from change.[8] This is related to Loss Aversion, which is itself a form of fear. Research shows that the fear of loss is so much stronger than the hope for gain that people must expect twice as much benefit from change as from the status quo if they are to be happy about it.[9] In organizations this leads to what has been called the La Brea Phenomenon: change is so difficult that the future must appear twice as good as the present in order to motivate people to change.

## WHY ENTREPRENEURS MAKE MISTAKES

At the same time that people undervalue the positive effects of change, entrepreneurs and entrepreneurial leaders invariably overvalue the new things they have developed. They say, "I know all the wonderful benefits of this new program because I developed them." An entrepreneur-specific form of the Endowment Effect is known as the Curse of Knowledge. Whatever the entrepreneur wants to do, it *was* "invented here," and he doesn't want to give it up. Moreover, the benefits are so obvious to the initiator that he fails to communicate them sufficiently and patiently enough to others in order to get them to change their minds. This is a major violation of the entrepreneur's critical need to communicate and change minds, as mentioned earlier.

As if this were not enough, change agents also undervalue existing systems and programs (I'm changing it; therefore it can't be any good). As a result, staff and colleagues wonder about the value of their work when the message they hear is, "All your hard work for the last ten years was worthless."[10]

Managing clashes of points of view and feelings is an absolutely critical task for the entrepreneur, but is also incredibly difficult because the innovator has the Curse of Knowledge!

## OTHER COGNITIVE ERRORS

Briefly, the Curse of Knowledge, the Endowment Effect, and Loss Aversion are only three of the major sources of error that can undercut the work of an entrepreneur. There are many other heuristics (mental shortcuts) that can trip up an entrepreneur, some disastrously.

> *Framing errors.* Kahneman and Tversky pointed out that the answer is affected by how the question is framed.[11] We ask "How should we institute these changes?" not "Should we make these changes?" or ask "How do we fill Bill's position?" not "Now that Bill has left, what skills and qualities do we need?"

> *Overconfidence.* A broader variation on the Curse of Knowledge. How sure are we that the proposed changes are the right ones? Are we sure it isn't just the Endowment Effect at work? I am a better than average driver and most of you are better than average drivers, but we can't all be better than average drivers. Skepticism is in order.

> *Expecting a perfect environment.* It is irrational to make critical decisions based on the idea that the change will prevent stressors and

disruptions like personnel changes, illnesses, new assignments, and late deliveries. Life will go on as unpredictably as before.

*Accepting only confirming evidence.* Symptom of the Endowment Effect. For example, Democrats believe PBS; Republicans believe Fox. This heuristic—"I think it is a good idea, therefore all the data looks good to me"—is a familiar side effect of the Curse of Knowledge.

*Underestimating randomness and reversion.* Investors should have learned from the Tulip Bubble in Holland in the seventeenth century and the Dotcom crash of the stock market in 2000 that today's high performer is likely to be closer to average tomorrow—or even below average. All things tend to revert to the mean over time, as housing prices did in 2008, with spectacular consequences.

*Confusing ability with good luck.* In the first decade of the twenty-first century, every rational observer knew that house prices could not continue to rise. Rational observers also knew that people without money cannot successfully buy and maintain houses, yet far too many people, including some very highly paid people, did not act on their understanding.

## COGNITIVE ERRORS, CLASS, AND CULTURE

These cognitive errors are bad enough in themselves but they are exacerbated by errors of thinking and understanding that are primarily cultural in origin. The *availability* heuristic is the tendency to look close to hand for examples, and what is closer than oneself? It is a grave danger for an entrepreneur to believe that "deep down, everyone is just like me." To believe that in a given situation others will act as one would act oneself is simply not true. Responses to change are bounded by class and culture, and in an increasingly global world, one needs to be aware of how these factors limit us and those with whom we work. For an entrepreneur to ignore these cultural differences is to risk failure.

Some simple cultural differences that cause a world of problems are things such as a sense of space. People from Mediterranean cultures, to choose a familiar example, tend to come close to people they are talking to and to punctuate their speech with gestures and perhaps touches. To many people of northern European descent this is famously threatening, and they don't like working with people whom they consider pushy. People living in large cities such as New York do not differentiate between what is appropriate in a public space versus what is appropriate in a private space to the extent that people in smaller cities do and may not, for example, bother to close their curtains to carry out certain private activities. In the workplace we find various culturally determined standards for such things as what is appropriate dress. Organizations may need to develop and apply dress codes when differing senses of what is appropriate lead to disagreements.

In the workplace, differing senses of time often lead to friction, as those who are invariably early to meetings fret and grow angry at those who are invariably late, but "early" and "late" are culturally determined. Arriving for dinner at the invited hour in Jackson, Mississippi, is socially important. In New York or London, being late is not only fashionable, it is expected. The entrepreneur's preferences can become the organizational norm, but it is inappropriate to expect others to intuit that norm. It must be made clear and reinforced in practice.

There are also cultural, generational, and gender differences in the sense of urgency with which people approach projects. In the eastern United States, one speaks of "a New York minute," of doing things "ASAP," of bosses who "want it yesterday." In the Hispanic world, *mañana* is good enough, and in the Middle East, *bokra* is like *mañana* but it doesn't carry the same sense of urgency. If the project is late, many Americans would fret, while the Frenchman or a Middle Easterner might say *tant pis* or *Malesh*—too bad—and a younger person might say "whatever." An entrepreneur who expects urgency in application to tasks may have to teach that sense of urgency.

We have all observed what appear to be male-female differences in how people approach and carry out projects, but the greater difference is that between inductive and deductive thinkers. Deductive thinkers start with a rule and apply it to individual cases; inductive thinkers start with the individual cases and try to define the rules that connect them. Both are perfectly valid ways of approaching problems, but they are opposite ways, and deductive and inductive thinkers are often in conflict along the way, though ultimately they may well get to the same place.

## Managing Risk

The would-be entrepreneur reading these pages may conclude that the primary risk to entrepreneurial activities is the same as the primary difficulty in all management: dealing with human behavior. This is broadly correct. With any luck, the framework I've provided for contextualizing these behavioral issues will help. These are normal, universal problems in any organization. They just pose a greater difficulty to new ventures than to continuing ones.

Problems in dealing with people undergoing change might be classified into three categories:

- 40 percent of them are based in human nature, the kinds of things described by behavioral economists;

- 40 percent might be based in cultural issues to which the entrepreneur must pay attention if not deference; and

- 20 percent are probably based on personal temperament, which the entrepreneur is probably stuck with. One can change behavior, but one is unlikely to be able to change temperament.

Given the trouble and the consequences, it might be tempting and a good deal simpler just to avoid risk and avoid being entrepreneurial in the first place. Unfortunately, the biggest risk of all is doing nothing. General Motors, Chrysler, and Ford are in deep trouble because they did not adapt their vehicle offerings to a changing market. Libraries risk losing share and support in the information marketplace unless they continue to change service and collection offerings. The report of the Library of Congress Working Group on Bibliographic Control advocates profound changes in the way libraries work and in the way they think about the work they do.[12] These changes will be threatening to many, and they will require a great deal of entrepreneurial work because at this time there simply are no fully defined models of the way to do things. But these changes are a risk the profession has to accept to remain responsive to current trends.

## Conclusions

The biggest risk to an entrepreneur is not external. It is the Curse of Knowledge, the mistake only the entrepreneur can make! Managers and leaders go wrong when they assume that a change is good just because they thought it up. Entrepreneurs must guard against the Curse of Knowledge by being rigorously honest, continually evaluating their direction to be sure that their information is accurate and their vision remains valid. Entrepreneurs must be humble, remembering that they are subject to exactly the same cognitive errors and cultural biases as their employees and colleagues. And entrepreneurs must be righteous. They are using someone else's money and changing other people's lives: it is a serious responsibility, and there are examples in the news every day of what happens when organizational leaders forget this.

Above all, entrepreneurs must try to maintain the high ground in conflict and avoid personalizing the issues. In the business world, those who disagree with the entrepreneur may be told "my way or the highway." In not-for-profits, we tend to medicalize the issues: "I'm OK, but you're not so hot," believing that disagreement with our ideas must come from a personality disorder. Both are reflections of the Curse of Knowledge.

Entrepreneurs must avoid treating as local and personal issues that are universal. In another organization in another situation, there would be different faces but the same problems.

The cure for much of this is to strive to understand why people act the way they do, to attempt to react to the behavior, not to the person whose behavior one dislikes, and to control the Curse of Knowledge by maintaining a dialog, by explaining as well as advocating, by listening and learning instead of continually talking. The answer for the rest lies in the entrepreneur anticipating internal and external, objective and subjective risks of failure and creating scenarios of possible responses to aid in reacting to them.

The good news/bad news is that we almost always overestimate the pace of change in the short run. There is more time than we think; one can take time to do it right. One almost always underestimates the amount of change in the long run. We cannot sit still.

## REFERENCE NOTES

1. *American Heritage Dictionary of the English Language*. 4th ed. s.v. "Intrapreneur," www.bartleby.com/61/61/I0206100.html (accessed 2 December 2008).
2. Brigham and Women's Hospital is a teaching affiliate of Harvard University accredited by the American Association for Accreditation of Ambulatory Surgery Facilities; the American Library Association has responsibility for accreditation of programs in library and information science.
3. Michael Kranish, "Yale Grades Portray Kerry as a Lackluster Student," *Boston Globe*, June 7, 2005, www.boston.com/news/nation/washington/articles/2005/06/07/yale_grades_portray_kerry_as_a_lackluster_student/ (accessed 1 December 2008).
4. Mark Landler, "U.S. Credit Crisis Adds to Gloom in Norway," *New York Times*, December 2, 2007, www.nytimes.com/2007/12/02/world/europe/02norway.html?pagewanted=print (accessed 1 December 2008).
5. Richard Thaler, *The Winner's Curse: Paradoxes and Anomalies of Economic Life* (Princeton, N.J.: Princeton Univ. Pr., 1994).
6. Steven D. Levitt and Stephen J. Dubner, *Freakonomics: A Rogue Economist Explores the Hidden Side of Everything* (New York: William Morrow, 2005).
7. Jerome Groopman, "What's the Trouble?" *New Yorker* 82, no. 47 (January 29, 2007): 36–41, www.newyorker.com/reporting/2007/01/29/070129fa_groopman (accessed 2 December 2008).
8. Richard Thaler, "Toward a Positive Theory of Consumer Choice," *Journal of Economic Behavior and Organization*, 1 (1980): 39–60 and Ziv Caromon and Dan Ariely, "Focusing on the Forgone: How Value Can Appear So Different to Buyers and Sellers," *Journal of Consumer Research*, 27 (2000): 360–70, http://web.mit.edu/ariely/www/MIT/Papers/bb.pdf (accessed 2 December 2008).

9.  Daniel Kahneman, Jack L. Knetsch, and Richard H. Thaler, "Experimental Test of the Endowment Effect and the Coase Theorem," *Journal of Political Economy* 98, no.6 (1990): 1325–48.

10. John T. Gourville, "Eager Sellers & Stony Buyers: Understanding the Psychology of New Product Adoption," *Harvard Business Review* 84, no. 6 (2006): 98–106.

11. Amos Tversky and Daniel Kahneman, "The Framing of Decisions and the Psychology of Choice," *Science*, 211 (1981): 453–58.

12. Library of Congress Working Group on the Future of Bibliographic Control, www.loc .gov/bibliographic-future/ (accessed 2 December 2008).

# Copyright, Fair Use, and Creative Commons Licenses

MICHAEL W. CARROLL

C reating and managing a library collection has always required some attention to copyright law. On the one hand, copyright law constrains collections because copyright owners use their legal monopoly to set the price for published works, and the exclusive rights under copyright restrain certain forms of sharing of the collection through photoduplication or other forms of copying. On the other hand, the deposit requirement under English and U.S. law has helped to build the collections of certain libraries (e.g., the Library of Congress), the first sale doctrine keeps the lending of copies in the collection outside of copyright's domain, and the fair use doctrine provides breathing room for a range of uses that enhance the value of a collection.

New challenges for managers of library collections have arisen from the fact that the digital era has brought with it an explosion of copyright events. The term *copyright event* refers to any action that entails the exercise of one or more of a copyright owner's exclusive rights to copy, distribute, perform, display, or adapt information. Some copyright events are infringing, and others are not. All implicate copyright law. Computers and other digital technologies must make copies to function, and some courts treat each of these copies as legally significant, thus causing copyright law to infiltrate almost every digital interaction.[1]

---

This chapter borrows from two prior works: Michael W. Carroll, "Creative Commons as Conversational Copyright" in *Intellectual Property and Information Wealth: Issues and Practices in the Digital Age*, Peter K. Yu, ed., Vol. 1, pp. 445–61, Praeger, 2007 and Michael W. Carroll, *Fixing Fair Use*, 85 N.C. L. Rev. 1087 (2007).

Explosions usually have violent consequences. The copyright explosion certainly has disrupted a number of industries and relationships that rely on copyright law. What is perhaps more interesting is how this radical expansion of the domain of copyright law has not led to chaos. Instead, a number of implicit understandings have grown up around digital technologies, and these understandings have led to norms and implied licenses that serve important coordinating functions. As robust as these informal mechanisms are, however, greater clarity and coordination can often be achieved when copyright owners explicitly designate which copyright events they consider to be permissible.

This chapter explains the problems that copyright law and uncertainty about fair use pose for collecting digital resources and how Creative Commons licenses respond by creating a pool of resources marked with open and machine-readable terms that invite collection and redistribution.

## COPYRIGHT

Modern copyright law presumes that one size fits all. Historically in the United States, an author or publisher had to choose to apply copyright when publishing a work. If a work was published without a proper copyright notice, it was dedicated to the public domain. Not all authors chose copyright for their work, and the public domain was immediately nourished. In addition, the duration of copyright protection was divided into an initial and a renewal term, giving authors a choice about whether they needed continued protection. Given that choice, most copyright owners did not seek renewal.[2] As a consequence, the manager of library collections should not assume that works published prior to January 1, 1978 are under copyright.

In the Copyright Act of 1976, which took effect in 1978, Congress took away these choices. Now the exclusive rights under copyright shower down upon authors as soon as they create their work without any action on their part to seek protection. Copyright applies to any original expression that is durable enough to be perceived or communicated in a fixed form. The standard for originality is quite low.

The one-size-fits-all approach applies to the scope and duration of copyright as well. With only a few exceptions, copyright law applies the same set of rights to any work, whether it is software, music, a motion picture, or the label on a shampoo bottle. In addition to the exclusive rights to make and distribute copies of the work, copyright law gives the author the exclusive rights to publicly perform, to publicly display, and to adapt the work. The renewal term is gone and the initial term lasts until seventy years after the author's death. This approach to copyright law assumes that all authors seek maximum legal control over their respective work.

The truth is far more complicated. Creators produce new works for a range of reasons, and they want different things from the law with respect to their creations. Some would like far more control over the use of their creativity than the law gives them. In contrast, other creators whose primary interest is in broad dissemination of their work, find that the automatic and far-reaching protection extended by copyright law impedes achievement of this goal because potential users or republishers are deterred by the need to seek permission for their desired use.

The emergence of the Internet greatly exacerbates the tensions caused by copyright law's one-size-fits-all approach. Digital technologies significantly expand the ordinary user's range of expressive power. One can now type-set and distribute one's book; record and distribute one's music; or direct, produce, and star in one's own film with relatively inexpensive and readily available tools. Younger users have embraced this power with gusto.[3]

Each of these works is subject to copyright. Indeed, nearly every Web page, graphic image, photograph, song, or video one encounters on the Internet is a work of authorship to which a number of exclusive rights are attached. These rights are *owned*. Thus, in the eyes of copyright law, the Internet, and particularly the World Wide Web, is a space populated by property and its owners. For these reasons, libraries are likely to be own-ers of copyrights as well as custodians and users of copyrighted materials. Library web sites, creative selections and arrangements of collected materi-als, and other graphic or textual materials are likely to be subject to one-size-fits-all copyrights. If libraries wish to share these owned materials with others over the Internet or otherwise, library managers will have to take affirmative steps to signal this desire to share.

As copyright's domain has expanded, increasing numbers of creators and users find that they do not fit within copyright's one-size-fits-all mold. Much of the creativity that digital technology enables is conversational in nature. Increasing numbers of Internet users take seriously the medium's interactive qualities. No longer does the user ask "what shall I read," or "what shall I listen to," or even "what shall I watch?" Increasingly, the Internet user asks "what shall I *do* with this?" As these users enter the Internet-mediated cultural conversation, they often want to do what they have always done. Comment on the news of the day, parody the politically and culturally powerful, and reinterpret the cultural texts that surround them. When done at the dinner table or among a circle of friends, these evanescent responses to contemporary culture draw no notice from the law. As this conversation finds its way to persistent and public form on the Internet, it enters the domain of copyright law.

Copyright law has some tools that can be used to facilitate conversational use of copyrighted materials. Limitations and exceptions to copyright permit a range of uses without the copyright owner's consent, and copyright owners can grant permission or a license quite easily. The fair use doctrine has become the most important of these.

## FAIR USE

The fair use doctrine is rooted in the truth that sometimes one must copy or otherwise use the expression of another to express oneself effectively.[4] Fair use protects a zone of expressive opportunity for criticism, comment, parody, education, and other socially beneficial forms of communication that might not occur if copyright owners were given complete control over how their works were used.[5] Fair use functions effectively only when users are reasonably confident in the legality of their use or when they are willing to adopt and defend a fair use position in the face of an uncertain legal standard.

Concerns about the problem of fair use uncertainty have intensified recently because fair use has been invoked in a variety of new situations. Wide distribution of digital technologies has greatly increased the domain of copyright law while also giving rise to a significantly larger pool of potential fair users attracted to the remarkable reproductive and adaptive power of these new technologies. The dispute over Google's digitization of large library collections is one of many signs demonstrating that, in the digital age, questions of fair use have taken on greater urgency. While the parties to that dispute appear to have reached a settlement, they persist in their disagreement about what fair use allows.

A fair user's uncertainty about the scope of her rights stems not only from the case specificity of the fair use doctrine but also from its codification in a nonexclusive four-factor test set forth in Section 107 of the Copyright Act.[6] Those familiar with copyright law are well acquainted with the difficulties in providing guidance under Section 107. Judge Posner, for example, has candidly admitted that only minimal guidance can be drawn from the four factors.[7] The treatise writers are in accord that the fair use doctrine produces significant ex ante uncertainty.[8] Indeed, when writing more pointedly in a legal periodical, treatise author David Nimmer examined many fair use cases and the findings on each of the factors and concluded that, "had Congress legislated a dartboard rather than the particular four fair use factors . . . it appears that the upshot would be the same."[9] That is to say, "the four factors fail to drive the analysis, but rather serve as convenient pegs on which to hang antecedent conclusions."[10]

As one might expect, potential fair users who seek to make public use of another's work often are deterred from engaging in a desired use by the uncertain scope of the fair use doctrine coupled with the high costs of litigation and the potentially enormous statutory damages that a court could award if it disagreed with the user's fair use judgment. Nevertheless, because educators and students must use a wide range of resources that lie within copyright law's domain, educational institutions have a strong interest in fair use clarification. In response to the uncertainty documented in Section 107 these institutions have resorted to a patchwork of strategies. For example, in the course of codifying fair use in the 1976 Act and subsequently, educational institutions negotiated with copyright owners, at times under the urging of Congress, to set forth rule-like guidelines that would establish safe harbors.[11] These guidelines do provide clarity for a subset of educational uses, but because these guidelines serve only as a floor, many colorable fair uses fall outside their ambit and remain subject to the standard four-factor uncertainty.[12]

Consequently, in higher education, university counsel and university librarians often must field a dizzying array of fair use inquiries and some have responded with fairly detailed guidance available on the Web.[13] Notable among these responses is the position adopted by the Office of General Counsel at the University of Texas, which has issued its own fair use rules of thumb.[14] In addition, the American Library Association employs a specialist responsible for fielding fair use inquiries and for providing general responses. Examples of the myriad endeavors plagued by fair use uncertainty to which she has responded include whether creating a computer program that explains the answers to math book problems is allowed; whether a student's freehand drawings of copyrighted characters can be put into a school magazine; whether student-made videos containing commercial music and video clips may be shown on a school's closed-circuit television station, and whether a library can put images of covers of recommended books on its children's website.[15]

These issues highlight the run-of-the-mill fair use uncertainty that darkens libraries and schools across the country on a daily basis. The transition to a digital environment manifestly increases the expressive costs of this uncertainty, which now touches upon systematic uses of copyrighted works. A harbinger for this development is the controversy that has emerged between the Association of American Publishers and the University of California at San Diego over the university's electronic reserve system.[16] The school has developed a new system through which students obtain required reserve materials online with a password rather than by going to the library to read books held on reserve.[17]

The publishers believe that this practice more closely resembles commercial course packs, which courts have found not to be a fair use.[18] The university believes that this use is the functional equivalent of a lawful analog use and that any suit by publishers would be futile and a public-relations disaster.[19] However, other institutions are less willing to rely on fair use for fear of litigation costs.[20] A range of other educational fair use disputes that have arisen, or are likely to arise, in the digital transition are further highlighted in the white paper: "The Digital Learning Challenge: Obstacles to Educational Uses of Copyrighted Material in the Digital Age."[21] As these emerge, demand for a procedure to clarify fair use will intensify.

In an environment of uncertainty, collection managers have to muddle through. In certain respects, fair use is a use-it-or-lose-it proposition because once a use becomes routinely licensed, it is less likely to be deemed fair when done without a license. Consequently, collection managers should understand that short-term risk management through routine licensing can lead to a diminished scope of fair use and increased licensing costs in the future.

## CREATIVE COMMONS

One means of reducing uncertainty and increasing the usefulness of collected materials is collecting materials under a Creative Commons license. Creative Commons is a work in progress, an ongoing natural experiment that began with a simple premise: in copyright law, one size does not fit all. This means there are authors who do not want the full set of rights automatically showered down upon them by the law. From that premise follows this hypothesis: if those authors were given a tool that is easy to use and that licenses back to the public some of the power to control the work that the public gave to the authors through copyright law, these authors would use such a tool. Widespread use of such a tool would create a commons, a pool of resources open to all to use in conversation and self-expression.

A Creative Commons license is such a tool. A Creative Commons license is a form copyright license that can be linked to via the World Wide Web. The principle of a Creative Commons license is to replace the default "all rights reserved" approach with a more modest "some rights reserved" approach that permits a variety of uses subject to one or more limitations that the copyright owner has placed on the work. In addition to the legal code, the license is described by a "human-readable" Commons Deed which identifies the key terms of the license and machine-readable meta-data that associate the Internet location of the licensed resource with the Internet location of the license document. From the user's perspective, the presence of a Creative Commons license answers the question, "What can I do with this?" by assuring that, subject to the license conditions, the user can: (i) copy the work; (ii) distribute the work; (iii) display or perform the work; and (iv) make a digital public performance of the work (i.e., Web casting).

A copyright owner seeking to offer her work under a Creative Commons license can do so by visiting the Creative Commons Web site (http://creativecommons.org) and selecting an appropriate license. Initially, the basic conditions that a copyright owner could choose to require from users were:

1. (BY:) Attribution. The creator requires attribution as a condition of using the creative work;

2. (S) NonCommercial. The creator allows only noncommercial uses of the work;

3. (=) NoDerivatives. The creator asks that the work be used as is, and not as the basis for something else; and

4. ShareAlike. Any derivation using the licensed work must also be released under a ShareAlike license.

These four options produced eleven possible licenses. However, early data showed that 98 percent of licensors chose the Attribution requirement, so Creative Commons made attribution a required condition of all licenses, which reduced the copyright owner's choice to one of six core licenses:

1. (BY:) Attribution (use the work however you like, but give me attribution).

2. (BY:) Attribution-ShareAlike (use the work however you like, but give me attribution, and license any derivative under a Share-Alike license).

3. (BY:) (=) Attribution-NoDerivatives (use the work as is, and give me attribution).

4. (BY:) ($) Attribution-NonCommercial (use the work for noncommercial purposes, and give me attribution).

5. (BY:) ($) (=) Attribution-NonCommercial-NoDerivatives (use the work for noncommercial purposes, as is, and with attribution).

6. (BY:) ($) (◉) Attribution-NonCommercial-ShareAlike (use the work for noncommercial purposes, give me attribution, and license any derivative under a ShareAlike license).

These options are layered on top of a basic template license. That template assures that the creator retains his or her copyright; affirms that any fair use, first sale, or free expression rights are not affected by the license; and gives the user a set of core freedoms to use the work so long as the user respects the conditions the creator has imposed. The license also requires the user to get permission for any uses outside of those granted, to keep any copyright notices intact, to link to the Web page on which the license is found, not to alter the license terms, and not to use technology (i.e., digital rights management) to restrict a licensee's rights under the license.

When the Creative Commons experiment was launched in December 2002, it was not known how large the set of authors interested in the some-rights-reserved approach would be. Available data do not enable precise measurement, but it is beyond question that the premise and hypothesis of this experiment are true. Within one year after launch, one could find more than 1 million link-backs to the Web pages containing the Creative Commons licenses.[22] It should be noted that link-backs are not really a count of how many objects are licensed under Creative Commons licenses—a single license could cover 100,000 songs in a music database, for example, or a single blog might have multiple instances of the license. In 2008, Creative Commons launched a metrics project that estimates the number of works available under a CC license. As of December 2008, the estimate was about 130 million works.

## CONVERSATIONAL COPYRIGHT: THE LICENSED COMMONS

As should now be clear, Creative Commons copyright licenses embody a vision of conversational copyright. Within this vision, creators or copyright owners seek to facilitate use of their expression for purposes such as dialog and education. In this way, Creative Commons licenses enable creators to reach a wide audience and save busy audience members the time and effort of seeking permission to share the creators' work. Catagorizing the numerous kinds of creators who embrace the vision of conversational copyright through Creative Commons licenses is well beyond the scope of this chapter, but a few examples might give the curious reader some sense of who the millions of license adopters might be.

At a time when numerous institutions of higher education looked at teaching materials produced on campus as a potential revenue source through distance education, the Massachusetts Institute of Technology (MIT) launched OpenCourseWare (http://ocw.mit.edu/OcwWeb/web/home/index.htm), a free and open educational resource for faculty, students, and self-learners around the world. By November 2007, MIT completed the initial publication of virtually the entire curriculum, more than 1,800 courses in 33 academic disciplines. Going forward, the OCW team is updating existing courses and adding new content and services to the site. To participate in the project, MIT professors agree to use a Creative Commons license for nearly all of their content. The license has enabled people all over the world, who have Internet access, to obtain, informally, many of the benefits of an MIT education. MIT hopes not only to spread its educational material, but also to promote the concept of opencourseware in general. At least ten other universities from the United States, Japan, and Viet Nam have launched opencourseware programs, indicating the concept's attraction.

Connexions from Rice University represents another educational use of Creative Commons licenses.[23] Connexions disaggregates learning materials by using small chunks (known as modules) as the basic unit of course material. Modules can be organized and linked into courses. Learning need not be linear and the use of modules can show "relationships both within and between topics" and that "knowledge is naturally interconnected." The goal of Connexions is to create a commons of high-quality, diverse content through grassroots collaboration, facilitated by use of a Creative Commons Attribution license. As of January 1, 2009, the site hosted 7697 reusable modules woven into 424 collections. Because of the open nature of Connexions, quality control is handled by allowing third parties to review the content, presented in the form of "lenses" that include ratings based on popularity, feedback by universities and other reliable sources, and peer assessments.[24] The modules are also being translated into several languages, indicating how Creative Commons facilitates not only dissemination, but also collaboration and community building in the educational context.

Finally, Berklee Shares is a collection of music lessons prepared by the faculty of the Berklee College of Music licensed under Creative Commons licenses. The goal is to provide free music lessons for the musical community around the world and to promote the Berklee College of Music. While not as broad in scope as MIT's OpenCourseWare or Rice University's Connexions, the Berklee use stems from the same philosophy that learning should be more widely available. It also demonstrates the potential to use content offered under a Creative Commons license for promotional purposes. Berklee Shares specifically states that one reason for making its content available is "to reach interested students and make them aware of the possibility and potential of a Berklee education."[25]

In addition to the professional creators who have found Creative Commons licenses useful, the largest group of license adopters has been the bloggers, video artists, and photographers who collectively produce what the popular press calls user-generated media (social media). Web sites such as Flickr, OurMedia, and YouTube have sprung up to host these creative works. Labeling these creators "users" is, in my view, a misrepresentation because they are creators in their own right. I prefer to think of this group as "because-I-can" authors for whom copyright law's one-size definitely does not fit. Asking these creators why they use digital technologies to create and to share their work, most will not respond that it is "for the money," or "for fame," but "because I can."

## COPYRIGHT AS A DIMENSION OF RELEVANCE

The Creative Commons experience points up an aspect of collecting information that has always been present, but is more pronounced with digital information and creates some risks and opportunities for entrepreneurship. The guiding principle for organizing and searching collections—whether library collections or a search engine's index of the World Wide Web—has been to search for topical relevance. From the user's perspective, the growth of the licensed commons points up a new dimension for measuring relevance—the use value of information found on digital networks.[26] Imagine, for example, an independent filmmaker is in need of some music to accompany a montage in a film. There is no time or budget to clear the rights to the music. A search for "Chopin" will sort the results not only by topical relevance—whether there is information, such as a music file, accurately associated with the search term—but also by "use relevance"—whether that information is available on terms that permit the desired use.[27]

This query into the use value of information is comprised largely of two components—one technical and the other legal. The technical question relates to whether the information is in a file format that permits the desired use, including whether the information is subject to technological protection measures. The legal question focuses on the copyright status of the work and whether a desired use is permitted. For those seeking to use information drawn from the Web, works available under a Creative Commons license have greater use relevance because the legal terms of use over and above fair use are clearly specified. Recognizing the importance of finding licensed content, Creative Commons developed its own search engine, and the Firefox Web browser provides a toolbar link to this engine.[28]

Some of the largest Internet companies now recognize the role that Creative Commons licenses play in signaling use relevance. Among search engines, Yahoo! released the beta version of the Yahoo! Search for Creative Commons on May 23, 2005, and Google enables searching the licensed commons through its Advanced Search capability. The site allows a searcher to choose among four criteria. He can type in keywords to find any topically relevant Creative Commons licensed content, or specify, "Find content I can use for commercial purposes," or "Find content I can modify, adapt, or build upon," or both. Significantly, Microsoft released a plug-in that permits users of the Microsoft Office suite to attach a Creative Commons license to their PowerPoint, Word, and Excel files.

Creative Commons licenses are described in machine-readable metadata expressed in the Creative Commons Rights Expression Language (ccREL).[29] The purpose is to anticipate and cooperate with the development of the Semantic Web. A detailed discussion is beyond the scope of this chapter, but the essential point is that with the right kind of metadata, machines can do a very effective job of finding, indexing, and acting on information available on the Web. Creative Commons supports the Semantic Web by providing those who adopt a license with metadata that enables a computer to recognize that a digital object (1) is subject to a copyright license; (2) that the license is a Creative Commons license; and (3) the identity of the applicable Creative Commons license.

## REFERENCE NOTES

1. See, e.g., *MAI v. Peak*, 991 F.2d 511 (9th Cir. 1993) (holding that every copy written to the Random Access Memory of a computer is a copy for the purposes of the Copyright Act).

2. Fewer than 11 percent of copyrights registered between 1883 and 1964 were renewed. See William M. Landes & Richard A. Posner, *The Economic Structure of Intellectual Property Law*, 212 (2003).

3. *Pew Internet & American Life Project, Teen Content Creators and Consumers* (2005). http://www.pewinternet.org/PPF/r/166/report_display.asp (accessed 3 January 2009).

4. *See. e.g.*, Emerson v. Davies, 8 F. Cas. 615, 619 (No. 4,436) (C.C.D. Mass. 1845) (Story, J.) (principal judicial architect of fair use doctrine recognizing that "[e]very

book in literature, science and art, borrows, and must necessarily borrow, and use much which was well known and used before").

5. *See, e.g.,* Paul Goldstein, *Fair Use in a Changing World,* 50 J. COPYRIGHT SOC'Y 133, 141 (2003) ("Some copyright bargains will fail because the copyright owner refuses to license a proposed use on any terms at all.").

6. 17 U.S.C. § 107 (2000).

7. *See* Ty, Inc. v. Publications Int'l, Ltd., 292 F.3d 512, 522 (7th Cir. 2002) (Posner, J.) ("The important point is simply that, as the Supreme Court made clear . . . the four factors are a checklist of things to be considered rather than a formula for decision; and likewise the list of statutory purposes."); *see also* William F. Patry & Richard A. Posner, *Fair Use And Statutory Reform In The Wake Of Eldred,* 92 CAL. L. REV. 1639 (2004).

8. See 4 MELVILLE B. NIMMER & DAVID NIMMER, NIMMER ON COPYRIGHT § 13.05[A][1][b] at 13-162 (citing e.g. Castle Rock v. Carol Publishing Group, Inc., 150 F.3d 132, 142 (2d Cir. 1998)); 2 PAUL GOLDSTEIN, GOLDSTEIN ON COPYRIGHT §12.2.2 at 12:34 (3d.ed 2005).

9. David Nimmer, *"Fairest of Them All" and Other Fairy Tales of Fair Use,* 66 LAW & CONTEMP. PROBS. 263, 280 (2003).

10. *Id.* at 281. Professor Barton Beebe's statistical analysis of more than 200 fair use opinions is consistent with this conclusion. *See* Barton Beebe, *An Empirical Study of the U.S. Copyright Fair Use Cases, 1978-2005: A Quick Report of Initial Findings for IPSC 2006* (draft Aug. 10, 2006) (on file with author) ("While I know of no statistical way to show that courts are indeed putting the cart before the horse when they engage in a Section 107 analysis, the strong evidence of stampeding is at least consistent with Nimmer's description.").

11. *See generally* Kenneth D. Crews, *The Law of Fair Use and the Illusion of Fair-Use Guidelines,* 62 OHIO ST. L.J. 599 (2001) (discussing these attempts and their drawbacks).

12. *See* Crews, *supra* note 11, at 668–69.

13. Stanford University Libraries, *Copyright & Fair Use,* http://fairuse.stanford.edu/ (accessed 3 January 2009); Copyright Management Center, *Fair Use Issues,* http://copyright .iupui.edu/fairuse.htm (accessed 3 January 2009); University of Maryland University College, *Copyright and Fair Use in the Classroom, on the Internet, and the World Wide Web,* www.umuc.edu/library/copy.shtml (accessed 3 January 2009); American Association of Law Libraries, *AALL Guidelines on the Fair Use of Copyrighted Works by Law Libraries,* www.aallnet.org/about/policy_fair.asp (accessed 3 January 2009); *see also* North Carolina Department of Public Instruction, *Copyright in an Electronic Environment,* www.dpi.state.nc.us/copyright1.html (accessed 3 January 2009) (guidelines for K–12 setting).

14. *See, e.g.,* Office of General Counsel, University of Texas, Fair Use of Copyrighted Materials, www.utsystem.edu/OGC/intellectualProperty/copypol2.htm (accessed 3 January 2009).

15. Carrie Russell, *Carrie on Copyright: A Tale of Two Textbooks,* SCHOOL LIBRARY JOURNAL, June 1, 2003, at 41 (Carrie Russell, the American Library Association's copyright expert answers questions on fair use, but states that her opinions should not be taken as legal advice); Carrie Russell, *Carrie on Copyright: Imitating the Masters,* SCHOOL LIBRARY JOURNAL, Sept. 1, 2002, at 39; Carrie Russell, *Carrie on Copyright: Television Test,* SCHOOL LIBRARY JOURNAL, Apr. 1, 2002, at 43; Carrie Russell, *Carrie on Copyright: Is It a Crime to Copy?,* SCHOOL LIBRARY JOURNAL, Jan. 1, 2002, at 41.

16. Scott Carlson, *Legal Battle Brews Over Availability of Texts on Online Reserve at U. of California Library*, CHRON. OF HIGHER EDUC., Apr. 22, 2005, at A36.

17. *See id.*

18. *See supra* note 11.

19. Traditional course reserves rely upon the first sale doctrine, 17 U.S.C. § 109 (2000), and/or fair use to make materials available to students. The ways in which fair use must substitute for first sale in the digital age is an important subject that lies beyond the scope of this Article; *See* Carlson, *supra* note 16, at A36.

20. *See id.* (quoting Jonathan Franklin, fair use scholar and associate law librarian at the University of Washington).

21. BERKMAN CENTER FOR INTERNET & SOCIETY, HARVARD LAW SCHOOL, *THE DIGITAL LEARNING CHALLENGE: OBSTACLES TO EDUCATIONAL USES OF COPYRIGHTED MATERIAL IN THE DIGITAL AGE* (2006) http://cyber.law.harvard.edu/publications/2006/The_Digital_Learning_ Challenge (accessed 3 January 2009). [Disclosure: I was a consultant for the project that produced this paper.]

22. A "link back" is a Web page that contains a hyperlink that points to the Internet location in question. Because use of a Creative Commons license requires a hyperlink to the Web page at which the license resides, "link backs" provide a rough measure of license usage.

23. See Connexions's Web site at http://cnx.rice.edu.

24. See *Connexions, Tour: Quality,* http://cnx.rice.edu/aboutus/tour/10.html (accessed 3 January 2009).

25. Berklee College of Music. FAQs. www.berkleeshares.com/faq (accessed 1 January 2009).

26. The idea of "relevance dimensions" is familiar to many who undertake quantitative study. See, e.g., Pia Borlund, *"The Concept of relevance in IR,"* 54 JOURNAL OF THE AMERICAN SOCIETY FOR INFORMATION SCIENCE AND TECHNOLOGY 913-925 (2003). www3.interscience.wiley.com/journal/104530966/abstract (accessed 31 January 2009).

27. Of course, there are also many others searching the Net for music files for personal use who consider the copyright status of the works to be irrelevant.

28. For those who use Firefox, the upper-right corner defaults to a Google toolbar, but it is a pull-down menu that permits use of other search engines, including those provided by Yahoo!, Amazon, and Creative Commons.

29. Hal Abelson, Ben Adida, Mike Linksvayer, Nathan Yergler, *ccREL: The Creative Commons Rights Expression Language,* Mar. 3, 2008. http://wiki.creativecommons .org/images/d/d6/Ccrel-1.0.pdf (accessed 3 January 2009).

# Moderately Risky Business

## Challenging Librarians to Assume More Risk in an Era of Opportunity

JOYCE L. OGBURN

One may not readily associate risk with librarianship; however, librarians deal with risk every day and in all parts of the profession. Acquisition functions, for example, include the risks associated with managing budgets and processes, producing appropriate audit trails, predicting and acting on pricing tends, and negotiating business terms and licenses. This is the area of librarianship where I began my career in the 1980s. Acquisitions trained me to think and act within a business context and to evaluate the risk of business transactions and relationships. The work had conservative elements that focused on avoiding potential problems, such as rigorously preparing for and facing audits or being careful to avoid any sense of unethical behavior with vendors or publishers. But my experience in acquisitions also emphasized that devoting unwarranted attention to exceptions and unlikely circumstances was counterproductive to achieving efficient and effective services.

In professional meetings acquisitions librarians discussed and informally assessed the risk of making business agreements with vendors and publishers. They debated the relative risk and value of putting all their eggs in one basket and incurring the potential risk of a vendor going out of business, versus using one primary vendor and reaping the benefits of higher discounts, more comprehensive services, and streamlined processing. Acquisitions librarians weighed the pros and cons and tried to monitor the health of vendors and used competitive bidding and contracts to mitigate the risks. Unfortunately the industry did experience the demise of Faxon, but despite this high profile failure, very few vendors have gone out of business. These strategies and risks are still in play and are accompanied by additional challenges deriving from the extensive use of technology and the rapidly changing environment of scholarly communication.

When offered the opportunity to tackle the topic of risk and entrepreneurship, the thought of librarianship as "moderately risky business" immediately leapt to mind. One might argue that this phrase describes the approach to risk that librarians may be prone to take. One might even argue that "conservatively risky business" would be more apt, not just because librarians are conservative professionals, but because they are perceived to be reliable, predictable, and good stewards, carefully guarding the fruits of research and teaching and of our documented culture for centuries. They also deal constantly with budget pressures without a steady means of revenue generation. Others may even chastise librarians for taking too many risks given the enormity and importance of their mission. With these constraints it is no wonder librarians can be risk averse. By overcoming risk aversion and sharing ideas for rethinking conservative approaches and tendencies, librarians can reap the rewards that risk can bring.

## ENTREPRENEURSHIP AND INNOVATION

Entrepreneurship is frequently associated with individual risk and individual rewards. Entrepreneurs are often viewed as people who single-handedly create and advance a vision through the force of their convictions, leadership, talents, time, and ability to develop an idea and secure investors. Despite the prevailing image, entrepreneurs do not succeed solely on their own—they find partners and build teams and organizations to accomplish their vision and ambitions. This process takes time, sweat equity, passion, and persistence—and it does not always lead to immediate or long lasting success.

Peter Drucker, doyen of modern management, offers sage perspective on innovation and entrepreneurship in several publications. In *The Discipline of Innovation* he tightly couples the two, stating "What all successful entrepreneurs I have met have in common is not a certain kind of personality but a commitment to the systematic practice of innovation," defining innovation as "the effort to create purposeful, focused change in an enterprise's economic or social potential."[1] Drucker advises that innovation be simple and focused—in other words, one should do one thing at a time. In his book length treatment, *Innovation and Entrepreneurship*, he dismisses the idea that entrepreneurs are characterized by a propensity for risk taking. He sees them as "opportunity-focused" rather than "risk-focused."[2] Librarians innovate and become entrepreneurs to serve users by advancing library programs rather than innovating for personal gain. Entrepreneurship by librarians is different from that of other faculty colleagues; librarians have an organization to run and are conscious of their service role, cooperative imperative, values, and the limited resources on which their services depend. They know that their entrepreneurial efforts must primarily benefit the organization rather than the individual.

Entrepreneurship may occur when an individual perceives a service need and a solution is either fostered within the organization or externally as a new business. In the library field *Serials Solutions* is one example of such an enterprise. Its founder, Peter McCracken, invested his time and energy in developing a service idea, and then enlisted the aid of others to help him pursue his goal of helping libraries manage their electronic resources at the title level. The idea was fairly simple and targeted to a real need. The development of *CONTENTdm* is similar. Greg Zick, a professor of electrical engineering at the University of Washington, perceived a need for managing digital objects and pushed to develop, test, and launch a product (*CONTENTdm*) now in heavy use among libraries. As entrepreneurs and innovators, both McCracken and Zick had the ideas and took the risk of turning those ideas into products and eventually new businesses. Librarians assisted them by risking their time, staff support, and other resources to test out and grow these new ideas into something tangible and successful for the community. Supportive librarians anticipated that these two emerging services would be important to achieving a more economical and sustainable digital library infrastructure and thus deserving of some risk on their part.

## RISK MANAGEMENT

Consider risk to have two aspects: risk taking and risk management. The term "risk taking" provokes an image of actions that are daring, foolish, and perhaps dangerous. Conversely, the term "risk management" sounds planned, calculated, and controllable. Librarians should think of risk in the latter sense, where risk is not eliminated but is understood and used to achieve desired results.

Organizational risk should be compared to financial investment strategies. Personal finance consists of a range of conservative, moderate, and aggressive strategies. Many people choose to invest in instruments such as money market accounts or certificates of deposit. These conservative strategies experience little volatility but actually may create risk by investing in instruments that may not keep pace with inflation. Conservative investors see consistent growth and believe that they are being wise and prudent in their investments because it is not obvious that a loss is occurring. While interest will certainly accrue, investments may slowly and steadily lose their value to the forces of inflation.

Investors who are willing to pursue a more aggressive strategy by investing in stocks may actually experience less risk in the long run because their gains will surpass the rate of inflation. A key factor is time; the longer people have to invest the more risk they can assume and tolerate, and the better off they are likely to be. If one is thoughtful and plans and manages this kind of risk, strategies that seem risky actually entail less risk and accrue more value if played out over a sufficiently long period. Diversifying investments and periodically rebalancing portfolios also reduce risk.

The economic crisis that materialized in 2008 seems to overturn conventional wisdom. Rather than rejecting what history has demonstrated, the situation highlights the importance of having a plan, understanding the risks one is taking, following fundamental principles, having a stash of reserve resources, and avoiding panic. Time is still on the side of the savvy investor and new opportunities will continue to arise even in the current market.

Risk-taking has not been a part of a typical profile of librarians, who have historically been rewarded for being conservative. If one considers change and competition to be like inflation, one has to wonder whether libraries are keeping pace and ultimately gaining tangible rewards for their prudence. In a short time frame losses are not noticeable. However, risk aversion means missed opportunities to invest in high value activities that may, in the long run, produce better results for users and garner more organizational power. What follows are some strategies librarians should consider for managing risk.

The first strategy is to assess the organizational "temperature" for risk, and then to ask what is at risk, and who will potentially benefit or suffer. The question of what is at risk is also critical. Is the risk a financial, reputational, safety, or legal one? Is the risk personal or institutional? Other strategies include creating policies and plans to mitigate risk. Grants leverage ideas and resources to accomplish a goal for which time and money are normally lacking. Seeking partners who share similar goals and have a concomitant level of commitment, along with the appropriate expertise may pay off better than working within a large general group. Partnership agreements can minimize risk if the partnership is new and a trusting relationship has not yet developed. In either case a group investment spreads risk among many, much as investing in mutual funds mitigates some of the risk of investing in individual stocks. Consortia, being composed of multiple libraries, may provide a pool of money that allows the group to assume risk that an individual library might shun either because of lack of resources or because the risk is too high.

Seeking out local resources is yet another strategy. A library in a university setting might consult the business school for help in developing a business plan. Depending on the policies and priorities of the institution, librarians may have access to venture funds to foster innovation and the pursuit of novel endeavors, leading to investments in new products, inventions, or business ideas. They may even be eligible to receive individual compensation from any revenue generated. For librarians, though, the lure of individual gain, large or small, generally is not a primary driver behind library innovation.

The size of an organization may influence risk management strategies. One might think that large organizations or those with substantial budgets have more opportunities or will tolerate more risk than smaller, less well funded organizations that normally have little extra capital or manpower for risky ventures. The latter could benefit from being part of a larger group, giving them the ability to call on more resources than they can muster on their own. The level of investment required by smaller organizations may be relatively less risky when underwritten by a group. Conversely, large organizations may be risk averse and resistant to change. The momentum of historic directions, habits and expectations can be very difficult to turn. Large groups may also rely on consensus, which may impede the ability to move quickly in new directions. Smaller organizations may feel they have less to lose (and everything to gain) and fewer people to consult, which can encourage agility and experimentation. While size and resources should be considerations, one should not assume that size is the sole determiner of risk tolerance or ability to optimize opportunities and manage risk.

## RISK IN THE LIBRARY ENVIRONMENT

Librarians have a hard time resisting order and completeness—this can be a great strength, but also a liability. Fortunately, many libraries have moved beyond seeking perfection in favor of reaching more people and providing faster delivery of services and resources. Librarians also tend to design processes for exceptions and let worst-case scenarios rule their thinking. How much risk is there that an exception will happen? By definition an exception is an unusual occurrence. When a mistake or adverse event occurs librarians may make more rules and convoluted "just-in-case" processes to avoid potential but unlikely reoccurrences in the future. They are actually creating more risk by permitting improbable reoccurrences to govern policies, processes, and procedures, and consequently are wasting resources that could be deployed to higher value activities. Librarians should design processes for the typical 98 percent of their work rather than the exceptional 2 percent. Then they can turn their attention to new problems and experiments.

Managing for exceptions afflicts more than librarians, as the history with license agreements attests. The fear of exceptions may cause publishers to lock down content in restrictive license terms and to invest a considerable amount of time and effort into crafting the perfect license. The risk of abusive use of databases or massive downloading of content may be low and sometimes little money or revenue is at stake. No doubt breaches and problems will occur, but one can question whether the consequences of an occasional problem are worth the effort of setting up draconian preparations and responses for all online resources. The developers of SERU, the Shared E-Resource Understanding, sought a new approach for arrangements that entailed little risk. SERU replaces a license with agreed upon best practices, achieving a mutually acceptable agreement by the parties involved without the need to invest heavily in lawyers and staff time.[3]

Librarians may also be trapped by fear of failure, believing that failure is unacceptable in their environment. While they hate to disappoint their users, they can be harder on each other than their users are on them. Librarians can develop plans that allow them to experiment and fail, learn, and do better the next time. They can line up support, set aside funding and space, and find grants and donors, as well as conduct research, assessment and pilot projects to provide a foundation for assuming risk. They should allow themselves the latitude to evaluate the long-term effects of new ideas and approaches and remember that time is in their favor in realizing investment goals.

Fear of success is another trap. Librarians may not want to risk being successful with new ideas, because if they are they actually will have to support their newfound success. Because formulating ideas is easy and managing transitions is hard, they worry that if their brilliant ideas work they will have to retool quickly and follow through with implementation. It is more comfortable to go along with familiar routines rather than risk something new. Successes deserve the same tending, planning and management as risk taking.

Librarians could profit as well from developing planning tools that include a risk assessment instrument by developing a risk tolerance assessment questionnaire similar to those used for financial planning. It would be interesting to know what kind of financial investor an individual is and what insights that knowledge would provide into how much risk someone is willing accept on the job.

Important and successful risks have indeed been taken by librarians including being at the forefront of the Internet revolution and exploiting it as quickly as possible. They were insightful in anticipating the value of being online and willing to risk plenty to move services and collections to the network level. Similarly, librarians have a long history of fiercely protecting copyright, fair use, privacy, and intellectual freedom, sometimes to great criticism and occasional scorn.

The recent trend toward mass digitization is one such example. Whether or not one applauds the Google 5 libraries for their decision to allow a commercial partner to digitize their collections, it is evident that these libraries took a deliberate risk when they decided to work with Google rather than conducting large digitization projects alone or in groups.[4] The decision was gutsy, and these libraries have taken heat for participating in this project. Nonetheless, they are shaping the environment rather than simply reacting to it or resisting a project that offered decided benefits, despite some troubling aspects. Librarians are learning more from this endeavor than they would have by sitting on the sidelines.

In tandem with pursuing risk, librarians have reduced risk and leveraged their resources by forming alliances or founding organizations such as consortia (e.g., OhioLINK, Greater Western Library Alliance), service organizations (e.g., the Center for Research Libraries, OCLC and LOCKSS), and even publishing ventures (e.g., BioOne). They have used these relationships to spread risk (and rewards) and to advance the goals of all participants, finding scalability, safety and economy in numbers.

## OPPORTUNITIES

It is worth remembering that Drucker says that entrepreneurs are opportunity-minded. Some new trends offer great opportunities for librarians.

Since the resources on which scientists rely have moved online, the need for more direct services provided by librarians has decreased. With requests for reference assistance declining, buying journals (when affordable) has become the main service libraries offer. In recent years scientists have been developing their own knowledge systems and methods of knowledge management, including informatics, digital libraries, software tools, preprint services, and data networks. What future can librarians envision with scientists?

Conversations about cyberinfrastructure and research computing have brought attention to changes in the conduct of science and the resulting service needs for conducting research, sustaining and capturing the non-published conversations of science, and curating the resulting data and the software that underpin science. For some time the National Institutes of Health have required researchers to deposit their data in an NIH repository and to do so in prescribed formats. Now, they have mandated that researchers deposit peer reviewed, NIH-funded research articles in PubMed Central. Simultaneously, calls for stronger data management plans in other federal granting agencies are growing. Working with data and other scientific information entails risk because it requires rethinking how librarians will exercise their roles as knowledge managers and stretches them to learn new skills or recruit new kinds of staff.

Managing scientific knowledge, one could argue, is as large a challenge as conducting computationally intensive science, and science fields are not the only ones being transformed. Digital technologies that have catalyzed the rapid changes in science are quickly infiltrating other fields. While librarians at relatively small, liberal arts institutions may not face the magnitude of the data management issues confronting librarians in larger institutions, their faculty and students will still be producing and using digital scholarship that requires tools, management, and curation strategies. When the world of scholarship is changing so fast and in so many different ways, worrying about mistakes that occur in processing print material, managing for exceptions, or creating perfect records must cease dominating the work of libraries, or they face the risk that their users will leave them.

Librarians can also provide assistance to faculty who feel pressured to start using more digital tools but who lack the necessary skills and may be reluctant to ask for help. Few people like to show their ignorance and many would welcome a safe place in which to learn. The library is such a place. This opportunity goes hand in hand with supporting digital scholarship.

As librarians contemplate risk-taking strategies along with imperatives to change, they should keep in mind the opportunities afforded by their strong campus relationships. They have a nearly captive audience and should take advantage of their proximity to their users who generally trust and respect librarians. However, users may not fully understand the transformation of library services that is underway and the new roles that are emerging for librarians. They may not want librarians to change, or may not be aware of the expertise that librarians can and should bring to the task of managing diverse knowledge resources. Librarians must be able to convince their users how these new roles build on historic traditions, values, missions, and strengths. Librarians and their users have many reasons for mutual reinvention and collaboration in common with their users and can help each other develop new services.

# THREATS

It is also worth bearing in mind that libraries face threats, often in the form of competition. At times libraries compete not only with each other but also with local information technology departments and commercial enterprises. Competition for staff includes technology and computer specialists, as well as newly minted graduates from information and library schools. Companies such as Microsoft hire information professionals. Even when libraries attract younger professionals, these librarians may become discouraged with the lack of support or enthusiasm to experiment and do things differently, creating a potential retention problem.

Libraries also face competition for the time and attention of users who create and use many knowledge resources other than books and journals. Like the sciences, many communities of practice in the humanities and social sciences are developing their own modes of sharing knowledge using digital technologies. Publishers may market products and services directly to an information technology unit or to academic departments when libraries can not afford these products or fail to see them as falling within their scope. The library role as middleman can easily be bypassed. Librarians must retain and nurture relationships with their users, even when they take uncomfortable new directions. Libraries cannot risk being usurped by others with money or influence who are not as well suited as librarians to manage scholarly products and primary source material.

Moreover, at present the users' evolving modes of work are creating demands that are difficult to meet. Scholars may be working inefficiently or may lack good tools. Unless librarians are on the mark, users may seek help from their colleagues or from other agencies. On campus, there is often competition for funding and status with the information technology department, especially now that much content and many functions and processes are digital. While librarians know that principles, practices, values, and decisions—not technology—are the heart of services, this may not be evident to others.

# RETHINKING ROLES

With entrepreneurship and risk management, as well as opportunities and threats in mind, how might librarians rethink their roles and services? Libraries still tend to define themselves around their collections. When librarians list their values and strategic areas, they often place building, organizing, and preserving collections right at the top. Is this shorthand for the same old approaches and formats, or are new methods and meaning being applied to this value?

Librarians who have begun recasting collection development or launching institutional repositories as a knowledge management strategy have taken steps toward reconceiving their collections.[5] It may be time to formalize a new definition for knowledge management that emphasizes the unique nature of higher education, which is open and collaborative, in sharp contrast to corporate knowledge management, which is closed and competitive. Business or corporate knowledge management emphasizes processes, business data, judgment, and actions of an organization. In my definition, knowledge management for higher education may be divided into two parts: 1) institutional business data—such as number of students, budget information, and credit hours—that contribute to managing the institution and are of primary importance to a single institution; and 2) mission-based scholarly products that derive from teaching and research, characterized by articles, monographs, working papers, theses and dissertations, and syllabi that have importance beyond the institution. Managers of university records and archives should engage with the institutional business model, while librarians should manage the scholarly products and assets, which constitute a collective research knowledgebase, by offering and preserving knowledge within an open and shared system that benefits scholars everywhere.

What is risky or entrepreneurial about redefining and taking on knowledge management? The new approach goes beyond traditional collection development with its attention to collecting resources by subject and from many sources. Instead it turns to the institution as the source of the material to be collected and managed. Librarians also have to sell the new definition, instill it into campus policies and practices, and live up to the promise of collecting, organizing, archiving, preserving, and providing access to a wider variety of materials (and potentially a greater amount) than they do at present. Librarians will have to re-evaluate their priorities and reallocate resources to undertake higher risk ventures that hold the promise of more value to their users. Otherwise they will risk alienating both users and the library's own staff who have come to expect libraries to provide traditional services with traditional roles for the employees.

To assist with knowledge management, it may be profitable to take the additional step of supplanting the broad construct of information technology with a new concept of knowledge technology—technology that supports the collection, analysis, synthesis, and presentation of research material. Knowledge technology could be construed to be interoperable, contextual, semantic, interpretive, integrative, evaluative, synthetic, extractive, and based in content derived from the academic mission. Documents and intellectual products would be smart and social, interact with each other, and be more independent of their creators, in effect living within a social network for "things" rather than people. Whether one accepts this concept as described, the point is that creating, managing and sustaining knowledge, particularly in an academic environment, should entail qualitatively different ideas and approaches from managing and transmitting information. If one assumes that knowledge technology can transform and is transforming the way in which scholars do their work, then librarian-entrepreneurs should grab the opportunity to envision, develop and apply knowledge technology to provide a richer research and learning environment for their users.

Library digital collections can serve as an example that benefits from the application of knowledge technology and knowledge management. Although all manner of digital collections have been created, they behave more like bits and pieces than cohesive collections. The catalyst that will turn these digital collections into compelling knowledge resources is often missing. Context is vitally important to understanding. Digital libraries contain images and texts that are disassociated from a context or that lack adequate explanatory and interpretive materials. These objects are static, in silos, and often presented unimaginatively and without adequate tools for manipulation. It will take time and ingenuity to craft products based in knowledge technology that can serve existing digital collections well. Libraries can allocate their resources and take risks to learn and apply knowledge technology to materials derived from the library's own collections.

The collaborative and open world fostered by the Internet offers innumerable opportunities for entrepreneurial librarians to stretch their wings and apply their prodigious talents. The Open Movement—including such concepts and products as open source software, open access, open courses, and open data—is an exciting and challenging development. Libraries have a lot to gain but could also experience real loss in the open movement—one could argue that potentially few have more to lose than libraries when open access becomes the norm. Rather than focus on potential losses, librarians should ask themselves whether they want the future of scholarship to be owned by the many or the few, to be open or closed, and then how they see themselves contributing to this future. An open future depends on active professional engagement and personal commitment, as well as institutionalizing the open movement. Librarians must be willing to expose themselves to the discomfort of advocacy, argument, criticism, and real change to be in the forefront of this movement. In fact, librarians have led the charge, along with many strong partners, on enacting legislation for public access to publicly funded research.

Librarians have able allies in the open movement. Many teachers and researchers are pushing to have their own works and those of colleagues in their discipline more accessible, read, linked, cited, and understood. Patient advocate groups are demanding more access to medical research. Libraries can also collaborate with a group I will refer to as competitive allies—those who work in information technology, museums, public broadcasting, and in a variety of not-for-profit organizations—with whom libraries can find commonality in the open movement. These organizations may also be seeking means to open up their collections and make their expertise more freely available, to bring more high quality and authoritative materials into the public arena via the Internet, and to help artists, writers, and other creators develop new forms of arts and sciences. Libraries and their competitive allies are all moving toward a more open approach and philosophy, allowing all of them to capitalize on this shift.

As libraries increase their presence in social networks, they may exploit these new modes of access to knowledge resources. Librarians at the University of Washington have embedded material and information from special collections in Wikipedia articles, which has heightened presence and usage.[6] Some libraries, such as the Marriott Library at the University of Utah, are managing iTunesU for their campuses by identifying and pushing content from many sources to digital places that students and the public are likely to visit. Recognizing that being embedded in the Web was a strategic advantage, OCLC took the risk of making WorldCat freely available on the Internet to channel users more effectively to member libraries.[7]

The development of social networks presents new research opportunities as well. For example, as folksonomies grow, librarians can explore and document how they develop and age. Are new formal or informal ontologies being born, and if so, how much use do they receive, are they being sustained, and how long do they live? Are folksonomies regularly updated by users or do they become stagnant over time? Are they really viable and do they accomplish their intentions? Pursuing this kind of research can go a long way toward understanding how trends in community "cataloging" are developing and whether new kinds of access are thriving. Rather than dismissing folksonomies, librarians should risk understanding or influencing trends in description within social networking tools.

## TIME FOR REINVENTION

Today's technologies, scholarly practices, and user behaviors have created new paths and relationships between libraries, scholars, readers, and publishers. The environment is breeding personal, professional, social, and organizational reinvention and reinvigoration.

Librarians can reinvent themselves and reinvigorate their libraries by assuming more risk and applying risk management strategies. They will have to experiment, shift, adapt, and interact within communities of interest that are quickly emerging, disappearing, and reappearing in new guises all the time. Rather than remain a buying club for traditional scholarly materials, libraries can become vital partners in creating and managing new forms of knowledge such as data, laboratory records, simulations, web sites, and digital arts that are significant components of contemporary scholarship. Librarians can not afford to cede technological support to other professionals, thus losing opportunities to couple knowledge technology with knowledge management and create a powerful foundation for future work.

In sum, to craft a new future while remaining true to the library's mission to find, preserve and make available the many stories of research, cultures, and people's lives and imaginations, librarians are urged to stop dwelling on the risk of experimentation. Instead, they should let go of control and step into unfamiliar territory. They must redefine their work; attempt radical new approaches; and seek new relationships to create exciting, rewarding, and risky services that have the potential to transform the lives of all those who create and seek out knowledge in its many forms. Perhaps then the profession will become the extraordinarily risky business it ought to be.

## REFERENCE NOTES

1. Peter F. Drucker, "The Discipline of Innovation," *Harvard Business Review* 76 (1998): 149.

2. Peter F. Drucker, *Innovation and Entrepreneurship* (New York: Harper Business, 1986), 139–40.

3. Karla Hahn, "SERU (Shared Electronic Resource Understanding): Opening Up New Possibilities for Electronic Resource Transactions," *D-Lib Magazine* 13 (November/December 2007), www.dlib.org/dlib/november07/hahn/11hahn.html (accessed 1 January 2009).

4. The original Google libraries are Harvard University, Stanford University, the University of Michigan, the New York Public Library, and Oxford University.

5. AAHSL Charting the Future Task Force, *Building on Success: Charting the Future of Knowledge Management Within the Academic Health Center* (Kansas City, Mo.: Association of Academic Health Sciences Libraries, 2003), www.kumc.edu/archie/bitstream/2271/68/1/Charting_the_Future_viewable.pdf (accessed 1 January 2009); Joseph J. Branin, "Knowledge Management in Academic Libraries: Building the

Knowledge Bank at the Ohio State University," *Journal of Library Administration* 39 (2003) preprint, https://kb.osu.edu/dspace/bitstream/1811/187/1/KBJAL.pdf (accessed 1 January 2009).

6. Ann Lally and Carolyn E. Dunford, "Using Wikipedia to Extend Digital Collections," *D-Lib Magazine* 13 (May/June 2007), www.dlib.org/dlib/may07/lally/05lally.html (accessed 1 January 2009).

7. "'Web Scale' Discovery and Delivery of Library Resources," OCLC, www.oclc.org/worldcat/web/default.htm (accessed 1 January 2009).

# Bibliographic Control 2.0?

## Entrepreneurial Lessons from Web 2.0

REGINA REYNOLDS and DIANE BOEHR

A continually updated service that gets better the more people use it, consuming and remixing data from multiple sources, including individual users, while providing their own data and services in a form that allows remixing by others, creating network effects through an "architecture of participation" and going beyond . . . to deliver rich user experiences.

*—Tim O'Reilly*

Collaborative, decentralized, international in scope, and Web-based . . . Data will be gathered from multiple sources; change will happen quickly.

*—LC Working Group on the Future of Bibliographic Control*

If the first description above sounds like a vision of the library of the future, that future is already here. The description is part of a *Compact Definition of Web 2.0* by Tim O'Reilly. The second description has similar elements and perhaps points to a similar future. It is a description of the future of bibliographic control as described in the introduction to *On*

This chapter was written by Regina Reynolds and Diane Boehr in their private capacity. The views expressed do not represent the views of or endorsement by the United States Government, the Library of Congress, or the National Library of Medicine.

Introductory quotes from Tim O'Reilly, "Web 2.0: Compact Definition?" *O'Reilly Radar*, (October 1, 2005), http://radar.oreilly.com/archives/2005/10/web-20-compact-definition .html (accessed 8 January 2009) and *On the Record: Report of the LC Working Group on the Future of Bibliographic Control*, (Washington, D.C.: Library of Congress, 2008), 4, www.loc.gov/bibliographicfuture/news/lcwg-ontherecord-jan08-final.pdf (accessed 7 January 2009).

*the Record: Report of the Working Group on the Future of Bibliographic Control* (*OTR*). The challenge facing the library community is to determine what changes are required in the area of bibliographic control to traverse the distance between where we are now and where we need to go.

Change is always a risky business and one that is especially challenging in the conservative arena of library cataloging. Cataloging rules seem to go through cyclic periods of simplification aimed at more reliance on judgment than on specific rules for every case, and yet as specific rules are added to the code over time, another round of pruning is required.[1] Calls for changes to cataloging practices are not new. They have been sounded for at least 60 years, from Andrew Osborn's 1941 article, "The crisis in cataloging" to the question raised (and answered) by Associate Librarian of Congress Deanna Marcum in 2004, "Can we rethink cataloging... in the world of Google? I hope so."[2]

On the other hand, cataloging practices have developed over a long period of time, and most of the practices followed by librarians have (or had) a good reason behind them. It is therefore frustrating to watch other communities grapple with metadata issues and then come up with pronouncements as if their ideas were brand new. In addition, catalogers raise valid warnings that when changes are implemented, care must be taken not to throw out the proverbial baby with the bathwater. It is necessary to recognize however, that the bathwater does need draining and to find a way to clearly identify the babies and protect them without reflexively saying this is the way things have always been done and that nothing can change.

If what we have been doing over the years has served us and our users well, why is it necessary to take the risk of changing our practices now? The answer is that the environment in which libraries operate has changed drastically. The development of the Internet and digital information has probably had as significant an impact on society as the development of the printing press. Libraries ignore this new environment at their peril. Web search engines and online bookstores are classic entrepreneurs. If they do not give users what they want, they will go out of business. Researchers and other users of libraries do not always have identical needs to those of Web searchers, but to believe that librarians know better than users what they need or want is patronizing. Thomas Mann, in comparing catalogers to health care professionals, says that health care professionals should not give patients what they ask for, because patients' requests do not match reality.[3] However, the idea of a paternal, all-knowing health care provider is an outdated concept. Doctors who do not listen to their patients and take their concerns and ideas seriously, in addition to relying on their own education and knowledge, are poor practitioners. This same concept may be applied equally well to librarians and their users.

## WEB 2.0 AS A MODEL

Recognizing that today's environment is defined by the Web, what can we learn from those who are studying Web 2.0? Tim O'Reilly defines the preliminary principle: "Web as platform."[4] The future of cataloging depends on how effectively the library community—from systems vendors to catalogers—responds to the key role the Web plays for today's information seekers. While it is doubtful that the library catalog was ever the first place that most people went when searching for information, in the past, aside from going to individual experts in the field, consulting printed bibliographies, or browsing the shelves of a bookstore, there were few other resources to which a person could turn. Now, however, there are many alternatives on the Web to which people turn first. If we want to expose people to the richness in library catalogs, then we have to expose the data in catalogs to Web search engines. Users were once satisfied with going to the library to make use of its resources. This is no longer the case. Users want the convenience of having library data at their fingertips wherever they are. O'Reilly references several Web 2.0 patterns based on work on programming language design done by the influential architect Christopher Alexander and adapts them into concepts radiating from the Web 2.0 core.[5] Many of these concepts seem highly relevant to bibliographic control and each of these will be examined in greater detail.

## DATA IS THE NEXT INTEL INSIDE

In the Web environment, data is a fundamental asset, and large masses of data allow one to do all kinds of things.

The obvious applications for a technology . . . aren't necessarily the ones that will have the biggest impact . . . . This is a key reason why companies like Google are increasing their data collection of all kinds (and their basic research into algorithms for using that data). As the applications become apparent, the data will be valuable in new ways, and the company with the most data wins."[6]

Consider the massive amounts of data in library catalogs and what a potential source of richness they offer to share and build upon. Creative ideas such as John Reimer's suggestion to map subject headings containing geographic names to coordinates of latitude and longitude to provide graphical search capabilities by place could also be combined with mashups like Google maps for even more interesting search and display possibilities.[7] The best ideas are probably those that haven't even been dreamed of and that may not come from the library community. Even the idea of traditional record structure may be obsolete in a world where everything can be taken apart, deconstructed and reconstructed.

However, this potential for creative use of data is lost unless the data that catalogers create is offered in a format that is Web-accessible or easily transferable to a Web-compatible format. Unfortunately, the format most widely used, MARC21, does not meet these criteria. MARC was a wonderful innovation that allowed widespread sharing of data among libraries, but it is almost 50 years old. Times have changed and cataloging data structure must change as well. It is high time that a standard to create and store cataloging data in a Web-friendly format is developed and this should be a primary goal of the leadership of the library cataloging community. While one entrepreneurial librarian might be able to come up with a workable scheme, it will take the community as whole to get a new standard accepted and implemented. Another alternative, one that will be mentioned in the section, "Cooperate, Don't Control," is to explore the use of multiple formats that might include a new primary format. Whatever the outcome of the potential "format wars," it is clear that change is needed.

As digitization projects are undertaken more widely, an increasing number of full text resources are becoming available. This combination of full text with existing high quality metadata offers another opportunity to create new and exciting ways to package and present information to users. To do this most effectively, catalogers need to stop thinking of every record as something that needs to be lovingly hand-created. There will always be material that needs to be dealt with on a one-on-one basis by a human, but much of the process of creating metadata can already be automated.

The amount of material being produced today already overwhelms human catalogers. Subscription packages contain thousands of titles, documents are being digitized on a massive scale, and the number of quality Web resources continues to grow. This material still needs to be organized and controlled, and the entrepreneurial cataloger must try to determine what tasks could be automated now with currently available technology. One crucial ongoing role of the professional cataloger will be to help programmers develop expert systems that replicate the mental processes used by catalogers, so that automated systems can produce similar quality results.

Because there was no alternative source of information, traditionally catalogers transcribed information from the items themselves in order to create catalog records. Now they should be able to take advantage of the descriptive data created by many publishers. Why would catalogers not want to let someone else do the less intellectually challenging work of transcribing data, thus freeing them to focus on what they do and know best: subject analysis, classification, authority work, and identifying relationships? Those who complain about the quality of publisher-supplied metadata need to consider that publishers have at least as strong a vested interest in the accuracy of the basic data about their titles as does a library because publishers have a profit motive. A misidentified book will not sell. If catalogers question the accuracy of publisher-supplied metadata, does the fault lie with publishers or with the cataloging rules? When catalogers have to tell a publisher that the title they have provided in their metadata (which matches the title printed on the item) is not really the title of their publication (as too frequently happens with serial titles), then something is wrong with the cataloging rules, not the publisher's information.

The current cataloging rules (*AACR2*) were clearly not written with automated processes or machine use of data in mind. The proposed new cataloging code, *Resource Description and Access (RDA)*, recognizes the possibility that some data will be ingested in an automated fashion but still refers to this process as transcription.[8] The level of descriptive detail called for in the current rules made sense when the catalog record was a true surrogate for a researcher who had to decide from the brief description if the item being described was really the item that was desired. Once identified through the catalog record, getting the item might mean going to the shelf, trekking across campus, putting in an interlibrary loan request, or maybe even making a trip to a geographically remote library. If a lot of effort would be needed to obtain an item, it was important that the description of the item be as detailed as possible. However, in today's world of mass digitization projects, the description needs to be sufficient just for discovery, and then with one click the user can view the item itself and confirm specific details such as imprint and pagination to determine if he has found the desired item. The level of effort expended by the user is minimal. Reducing the level of descriptive detail in a catalog record in today's environment would still conform to Ranganathan's principle of "Save the time of the user."[9]

However, cataloging rules designed to allow more machine processing may require additional data in some other areas of the record. Many have noted that the role of individuals and bodies recorded in the bibliographic record should not have been eliminated and that omission will become more critical as Functional Requirements for Bibliographic Access (FRBR) is more fully implemented. To enable better automated assistance with authority control, it would be useful to include authors' degrees and affiliations either as part of the statement of responsibility or in a well-linked and well-parsed authority record. If *RDA* is adopted and catalogers are no longer limited to the rule of three, and if more information about authors is needed in catalog records, then it becomes even more imperative that information be acquired in an automated fashion since no one has the time or resources to locate and transcribe all of this data manually.

With large amounts of digital data such as prefaces, summaries, and tables of contents, as well as full text, catalogers can also begin to explore automated assignment of subject headings using controlled vocabularies. Extremely large databases can be mined for computational indexing with astonishingly good results. If catalogers work hand-in-hand with programmers, they are likely to come up with better strategies and term mappings than if each community works independently. This strategy is not effective for materials in all subject areas, but it is certainly most feasible in areas such as the hard sciences that use fairly narrow vocabularies and unambiguous terms. Risk can be minimized by using new techniques where most appropriate. Progress will not be achieved unless catalogers focus on the instances where something will work, instead of concentrating on concepts or practices that do not work. Too often people condemn an idea because they can think of 5 percent of cases where it wouldn't work, rather than saying "let's apply this to the 95 percent of the cases and worry about the outliers later." There is an unstated assumption that work done by machines is of poor quality, while the work done by humans is perfect. However, this is obviously not true. Almost every week on the electronic list AUTOCAT (http://listserv.syr.edu/archives/autocat.html) messages are posted pointing out incorrect or nonsensical subject headings that were assigned by a cataloger, and these mistakes do not result in calls to stop human cataloging. However, if a machine assigns an incorrect term on one out of 100 records, many consider that attempt to automate subject assignment as a failure.

## THE LONG TAIL

The Long Tail is a concept developed by Chris Anderson that postulates that if the distribution channel is large enough, products in low demand or with low sales volume can collectively make up a market share that rivals or exceeds the relatively few high volume products. On a graph charting popularity vs. inventory, the total volume of low popularity items exceeds the volume of high popularity items.[10] In the publishing industry, the stock of chain bookstores consists largely of popular items on currently popular topics, and smaller, independent bookstores can only afford to stock a limited number of specialized materials. On the other hand, Amazon.com can boast of its "millions of books new and used" and can say of their sales pattern, "We sold more books today that didn't sell at all yesterday than we sold today of all the books that did sell yesterday:"[11] Amazon.com is an example of the power of the long-tail.

Libraries are a very rich source of "long tail" material of enormous potential value to their users, and the value of the cataloging is greatly increased when "low popularity" items are easily accessible to users. For example, many libraries have already found that putting their government documents into the catalog balloons the circulation of this material. In an information-rich world, the library's market share is likely to come from the unique treasures in its collections and that is where much effort should be focused if the library is to remain relevant. One of the five main recommendations of the Library of Congress Working Group on the Future of Bibliographic Control was "Enhance Access to Rare, Unique, and Other Special Hidden Materials." The report included this very specific recommendation to the entire community: "Direct resources to support the discovery of these materials, including resources freed by the institutions from economies realized in other areas."[12]

The long tail material in libraries is often literally buried in the collections. Far too frequently there is no metadata at all for this material. Users have no idea the material exists because there are no records for it in the catalog or in A–Z listings on the library's Web site. Curators and reference librarians may know where the material is and how to access it, but researchers must come to the library and be lucky enough to speak with these people to find out that it even exists. As good entrepreneurs, librarians must ensure that their collections do not contain hidden treasures—all resources must have some level of cataloging so that users can access the complete range of materials. Rather than having cataloging staff revise and polish records for common commercial titles that can be found in hundreds of libraries (especially since so much of this material could be cataloged in a more automated fashion), time and energy should be spent cataloging the unique and rare materials in library collections. Ideally, where copyright allows, libraries should also be digitizing this material to make it widely available. If digitization is impossible, at least the metadata for these items needs to be exposed on the Web.

The long tail model posits small but continual use of these "less popular" items. Because of the high value and enduring potential of the rare and unique items in library collections, library staff must ensure that these items can be identified and retrieved well into the future. Therefore, the records must be full enough and standardized enough to be useful and usable over long periods of time. The challenge is to find the balance between the economics of controlling these items in the best possible way and letting them languish in uncontrolled backlogs. Entrepreneurial approaches may be the way to cut this Gordian knot.

# THE PERPETUAL BETA

After attending a presentation on the report of the LC Working Group, Donald Lindberg, library director of the National Library of Medicine, said to one of the report's authors, "You're doing a good job here of trying to make the bicycle go faster—but what you should be doing is inventing an airplane. You need to throw out all the existing rules."[13] Ongoing development is another key characteristic of Web 2.0. One of the memes in the "meme map" in O'Reilly's article "What is Web 2.0" is the notion of "perpetual beta"—that ideas and applications are always under development and evolving, an entrepreneurial attitude that may be applicable to the bibliographic control environment.[14] It is probably too risky to just say "Throw away all the cataloging rules." While we support developing the airplane—and soon—it is also worth noting that both the bicycle and the airplane use wheels, and there is no need to reinvent the wheel. Many cataloging practices have a long and well-proven track record. Practices have changed over time to accommodate different formats, user needs and expectations, but there are some bedrock principles that remain consistent over time. As professionals, librarians need to define what those principles and elements are and then ensure that they are applied consistently. This needs to done based on serious evidence-based research, rather than on hunches and gut feelings. Practices that were developed for reasons that are no longer relevant must not be unnecessarily retained. How many of the existing rules in *AACR2* are based on the needs and limitations of the 3" × 5" card? How many of those rules were carried over into *RDA*? When will the time be taken to seriously examine rules and practices, if not now?

It is time to put the *science* back into *library science*. The LC Working Group called on the Library of Congress and the bibliographic community to "Build an evidence base" and elaborated on that challenge in a series of recommendations such as "encourage ongoing qualitative and quantitative research (and its publication) about bibliographic control, for various types of libraries and over a protracted period of time."[15] Has the time come for all library schools to include a research requirement? Under present circumstances, this may seem an unattainable ideal, since many schools don't even require a cataloging class. However, requiring a basic understanding of the principles and practices of bibliographic control, as well as some research experience, would seem to provide crucial survival skills not only for cataloging professionals but for the profession as a whole.

One characteristic of research is that experiments are not always successful. As Marshall Keys states in the introductory chapter of this book, "Entrepreneurs often fail, but unlike most of us, they accept failure, learn the appropriate lessons, and move on."[16] Supposedly, Thomas Edison needed 10,000 tries to get the light bulb right. Library environments don't easily support failure. The culture of perfection is one of the challenges that cataloging has to overcome and that same culture often extends to avoidance of all kinds of errors and failures. Perhaps the idea of the perpetual beta will help move libraries forward: the catalog record does not have to be perfect the first time; in cooperative settings others will come along and correct or augment it. New formats, rules, and processes can also be thought of as evolving; perfection is not required for every entrepreneurial effort to remain relevant in the digital environment. Rather, lessons can be taken from what Web entrepreneurs do: get projects out there and let their strong and weak points come to the fore, explaining problems as "bugs" or "glitches" to be worked out in the next release.

## COOPERATE, DON'T CONTROL

In difficult economic times, where companies and institutions are struggling just to survive, cooperation becomes an increasingly important strategy. The Web 2.0 design pattern "Cooperate, Don't Control" is based on the work of Christopher Alexander and is couched in terms of Web architecture. Alexander describes his concept this way: "Web 2.0 applications are built of a network of cooperating data services . . . re-use the data services of others . . . as well as 'models that allow for loosely-coupled systems.'"[17] The advice to cooperate rather than control seems applicable in today's library environment where cooperative efforts need to be extended and expanded and where overly tight control can stymie these efforts.

In an online presentation entitled "What if we were starting from scratch," Owen Stephens seems to suggest a similar approach by calling for an entirely new infrastructure based on Tim Berners-Lee's requirement for a global hypertext system that allows small isolated systems to grow and merge without requiring any central control or coordination.[18] The LC Working Group also suggests a broader and more loosely conceived model for cooperation among libraries and others in the information community by emphasizing that "bibliographic control [is no longer] the domain only of libraries, publishers and database producers . . . . The continued sharing of effort will be one of the keys to the future success of libraries . . . . Moreover, libraries will need to collaborate not just with each other but with other organizations as well."[19]

Cooperation always involves giving up some control—the challenge is to determine what control to give up and what to retain. An example from the early days of CONSER (the 35 year-old cooperative program for serials cataloging) is instructive. For the first eleven years (1973–1984), LC retained complete control over every CONSER record that was produced. LC had sole responsibility for establishing name headings and creating authority records as well as for record "authentication," a process that consisted of reviewing records for accuracy, authoritativeness of headings, and conformity to cataloging rules as interpreted by CONSER documentation. Even after the right to create authority records was extended to all CONSER participants in1981, LC still attempted to authenticate each record before it was distributed to MARC subscribers but backlogs of records waiting to be authenticated accumulated.[20] Once LC relaxed its control, the bottleneck caused by the review process loosened and CONSER production and membership grew significantly. The opening of authority record creation via establishment of the NACO program further changed the cooperative landscape dramatically, ushering in the current state of cooperative cataloging in which over 600,000 new and changed authority records were contributed to the cooperative authority file during 2007/2008.

The degree of tight control formerly exercised by the Library of Congress may seem quaint by today's standards, yet there remain many areas where lessening of control—by LC as well as by the other organizations such as the American Library Association (ALA), the Joint Steering Committee (JSC), and the Machine-Readable Bibliographic Information Committee (MARBI), to name a few—might allow for even more interoperability, cooperation, and productivity. Analysis is needed concerning the areas where tight control of the mechanisms of bibliographic record production is beneficial and where such control is strangling growth, partnerships, and timeliness.

Roy Tennant, the author of *Library Journal's* "Digital Libraries" column, questions the very concept of bibliographic control: "I no longer think 'control' is either achievable or even desirable. We have entered the age of 'descriptive enrichment' and we'd better get bloody well good at it."[21] Many of the rigid controls for describing resources such as the rules for capitalization, exact transcription, and abbreviation that have been characteristic of library cataloging codes at least since Cutter's time need further examination and modification.

To assist with the important goals of collocation and disambiguation, there currently are very complex rules for establishing name headings, and only one form of a name is considered to be "correct." However, in an international environment of shared catalog records, it would be much more effective to focus on establishing personal and corporate name registries, where catalogers could identify which entities are actually the same or different, assign unique identifiers to these entities, and allow individual libraries to display these headings in whatever form works best for their users—whether that be in English or in other languages, or as transliterated headings or vernacular scripts.

In the same vein, elaborate rules and practices for constructing subject headings, limitations on use of subject access points from non-library thesauri, and "bibliographic instruction" (we'll teach you how to understand our records rather than creating user-friendly ones) are all examples of areas where tight control of bibliographic record creation needs to be examined and unnecessary controls either loosened or discarded.

The primary bibliographic format, MARC, is another area where the cataloging community has maintained control—a control that began as needed standardization—but one that many now believe presents a barrier to interoperability and cooperation with those outside the library community. While some feel MARC can easily be converted to whatever format a partner might use, others share the view of the LC Working Group on the Future of Bibliographic Control that "the library community's data carrier, MARC, is based on forty-year-old techniques for data management and is out of step with programming styles of today. No community other than the library community uses this record format, severely compromising its utility to other communities as a data transmission tool."[22] Replacing MARC would be risky—millions of records and multitudes of library systems in the U.S. and elsewhere would be affected, but there are risks to not taking this step. Is a single replacement format essential? Or is accommodation for multiple formats possible?

Another major area where cooperation would be beneficial is reflected in the LC Working Group's recommendations for dealing with some of the challenges of bibliographic control by holding community discussions, meetings, or working groups to:

- "address costs, barriers to change, and the value of potential gains arising from greater sharing of data" and "promote widespread discussion of barriers to sharing data" (1.1.4.1 and 1.1.4.2);

- "bring together other communities working on problems of identification of authors and other creators" (1.3.2.2);

- "work with interested entities such as PCC, ARL, professional organizations, publishers, etc. to plan transition to new distribution of [cataloging] responsibilities" (1.2.2.3);

to name only a few. Although the library profession prides itself on cooperation (cooperative acquisitions programs such as PL 180, cooperative cataloging programs such as CONSER, NACO, and BIBCO and library consortia have existed for decades) clearly more and broader cooperation, as well as less rigid control, is needed.

## HARNESSING COLLECTIVE INTELLIGENCE

One of the most surprising phenomena associated with the early Web, according to a 2005 *Wired* article entitled "We are the Web," was the explosion of user-contributed data. That article stated, "What we all failed to see was how much of this new world would be manufactured by users, not corporate interests."[23] Contrary to the fears of early information providers (the media and others) about how they could possibly provide the volumes of data the Web seemed to demand, ordinary people became contributors, many of them uploading more data than they downloaded. This phenomenon has only increased. Certainly one of the most pervasive and successful aspects of Web 2.0 is its unexpected success in both engaging users and taking advantage of users' willingness—even eagerness—to participate and contribute in ways that as O'Reilly says, "[build] value as a side-effect or ordinary use of the application."[24] Additionally, users have become "prosumers" (producers as well as consumers) and seem to delight in providing content for nothing more than the chance to interact with those "out there." Wikipedia (user-contributed/user-edited articles), eBay (user feedback), Amazon.com (reviews and user data), You-Tube (user-created videos), and Flickr (user-created photographs), to name only some obvious examples, are examples of the content and value that users add. None of these sites could exist without intensive user participation.

Libraries—institutions that have engaged and inspired passionate users for centuries—are increasingly making forays into harnessing the considerable collective intelligence of their users. For example, next generation catalogs can take advantage of circulation data to recommend similar titles and search data to present results ranked by relevance. But active, expert library communities should present catalogers with additional opportunities to more directly harness their collective intelligence. The incorporation of user-contributed data into library catalogs still seems in its early stages. Is this because librarians covertly feel superior to their users? Let us hope not. Or is it because they fear the risk of learning that they do not always have all the answers? Perhaps the question of control also applies here. Although harnessing collective intelligence presents multiple and risky challenges, it also has the potential to provide significant rewards and may even be an essential survival strategy in today's environment where users turn to Wikipedia far more often than to *Encyclopedia Britannica*. Not surprisingly, an article in *TechCrunch* states, "According to Comscore, for every page viewed on Britannica.com, 184 pages are viewed on Wikipedia (3.8 billion v. 21 million page views per month)."[25] Even before librarians can enlist users in providing "intelligence" in the form of tags, reviews, or recommendations, they first need to engage users more fully. Too often librarians try to change users to conform to their perceptions about how they *should* behave. But, as Karen Schneider—who blogs as the Free Range Librarian—proclaims, "the user is not broken." In fact, she says "the user is the sun," and "you cannot change the user but you can transform the user experience to meet the user."[26] Libraries need to remove the barriers to user engagement—such as unfriendly OPACs—and may need to meet users more frequently where they congregate—on blogs, on YouTube, using RSS feeds and Wikis, or whatever the next distribution channel might be. At the very least, librarians need to determine where users want librarians to meet them, since a University of Michigan user survey seemed to indicate that almost half of the students surveyed did not want the library in "my space."[27] Alternative delivery mechanisms for both metadata and data include OAI harvesting, as well as methods that expose metadata to search engines since the use of search engines such as Google is a primary search avenue for today's users.

A significant barrier to a good user experience is the typical library OPAC. In a study of student information-seeking cited by Lynn Silipigni Connaway, she quotes a student as saying, "I stay away from the library and the library's online catalog."[28] Such student attitudes towards the library catalog no doubt cause many a library administrator to question the expense and value of cataloging when the catalog should bear as much, if not more, of the blame. Whether Google has the best search interface may be debatable, but what is not debatable is that Google's single search box, use of spell correction, suggestion of alternatives and arrangement of responses by user popularity has come to define the user search experience. Catalogers ignore these user expectations at their peril. After decades of enduring abysmal OPACs, libraries now have some choices in "next generation" interfaces such as AquaBrowser, Endeca, and the University of Rochester's development of the eXtensible catalog. These interfaces are characterized by such features as faceted browsing, stemming, tag clouds, relevancy ranking, "did you mean" responses to incorrect spelling, and the capability for "one-stop searching" of various library resources. Will these catalogs encourage more users, especially undergraduate students, to become users of library catalogs? Let us hope it is not too late.

The second challenge for libraries attempting to harness collective intelligence is to develop ways that users can enrich and extend the bibliographic descriptions catalogs provide by adding their perspectives and expertise. The LC Working Group urged the entire library community to "integrate User-Contributed Data into Library Catalogs."[29] Although controlled subject vocabularies such as LCSH make for well-ordered catalogs and allow searching by subject regardless of the language of the work, these vocabularies often do not mesh with users' perceptions. Melissa Rethlefesen wrote that "tagging, as with del.icio.us and other social bookmarking tools, lets libraries label books in ways that make more sense to patrons than traditional subject headings."[30] Rather than substituting user tags for controlled vocabularies, an obvious step is to supplement controlled vocabularies with tags. Will there be enough incentive to induce large-scale user tagging on library bibliographic descriptions, or will it be more effective to export tags from sites such as Library Thing via mechanisms such as Library Thing for Libraries? Questions on this matter are just beginning to be formulated.

Although user tagging appeals to public, school and academic libraries wanting to demonstrate their openness to Web 2.0, user-tagging works best in environments that are larger than those of most individual libraries. Unlike traditional library catalogs that become more difficult to search the larger they are, when it comes to collective intelligence, bigger is better. Tagging by a few on a small database can produce skewed results, but the larger the number of taggers and the larger the database, the more the "wisdom of crowds" comes into play. This is surely an area where large library databases such as that of the Library of Congress, or WorldCat, or the ISSN Portal can benefit from their size rather than suffer (as often happens) from enormous search results arranged in less-than-useful order (e.g., chronological by date of record input).

Libraries must recognize that tags are going mainstream. Prominent in *Time*'s 2008 "Man of the Year" issue is a section entitled "Barack Obama on Flickr." The introduction to the section reads "The historic 2008 election inspired thousands of people around the world to post their Obama-themed photography and art on the image-sharing site Flickr. Here is the best of the 100,000 images TIME examined."[31] Without user tags, culling even 100,000 photos from the 3 billion images Flickr contained as of November 3, 2008 would have been impossible. On its "About Flickr" page, is a "metadata for dummies" summary of user tagging that begins: "We want to enable new ways of organizing photos and videos" and after explaining how family, friends, and Flickr users can add tags to photos and videos, the summary concludes, "as all this info accretes as metadata, you can find things so much easier later on, since all this info is also searchable."[32] This is a description of user tagging in a nutshell!

In December 2008, the Library of Congress released a report that highlights the success of its Flickr Pilot Project. Between January 16, 2008, when LC's Flickr page debuted, and October 23, 2008, there were 10.4 million views of the LC photos on Flickr and 67,176 tags were added by 2,518 unique Flickr accounts. LC was able to use the identifications, corrections, dates, and links added by Flickr members to the LC photos posted on Flickr to augment more than 500 records in LC's own Prints and Photographs Online Catalog. There was also a significant increase in views and downloads from the LC site of images that corresponded to those that were uploaded to Flickr. The pilot team recommended that "LC continue to participate in The Commons [the area of Flickr where photos that have no known Copyright restrictions are held] and explore other Web 2.0 communities."[33]

Other projects in which user tags are augmenting library-supplied metadata include the University of Pennsylvania's Penn Tags; OCLC's addition of tagging for users of WorldCat.org; and the University of Michigan's MTagger capability.[34] Michigan's Ken Varnum posted an announcement on *RSS4Lib* in which he states "MTagger brings a social component to research that we have not previously had. It will allow users to share knowledge about library resources with each other, to enable quick-and-dirty subject guides to be produced, and—we hope—to bring researchers together via their individual tag clouds."[35] Catalogers may be facing an exciting future in which they participate in more synergistic ways with library users to achieve a more user-centered vision of bibliographic control.

## PLAY

Roger von Oech, writer and speaker on creativity and author of *A Whack on the Side of the Head*, said, "Necessity may be the mother of invention, but play is certainly the father."[36] Since the ability of play to foster creativity is well known, it is not surprising that "play" shows up on the Web 2.0 "meme map" developed by O'Reilly Media.[37] Most likely many libraries would find that incorporating "play" into their position descriptions or performance plans would be risky, but nevertheless they might be surprised at the positive results. Surely survival in the digital environment challenges libraries to be creative in a way that no previous environment has done. In *Whack*, Von Oech identifies ten characteristics that inhibit creativity.[38]

- The Right Answer
- That's Not Logical
- Follow the Rules
- Be Practical
- Play Is Frivolous
- That's Not My Area
- Avoid Ambiguity
- Don't Be Foolish
- To Err Is Wrong
- I'm Not Creative

Do these sound like familiar phrases and attitudes in library culture? Research by von Oech and others indicates that creative ideas emerge much more easily when people have the freedom to play with ideas and when they are in a non-judgmental environment where they don't have to be afraid of making mistakes or being wrong.[39] Albert Einstein is known for his great intellect and his ability to encompass mind-numbing concepts such as relativity. But Einstein also had a playful side, as evidenced by the famous picture of him on his seventy-second birthday, sticking his tongue out at early paparazzi who would not leave him alone. A description of the background to this picture in *Famous Pictures: The Magazine* indicates that Einstein liked this picture so much he sent it to friends as a greeting card.[40] The article also recounts Einstein's response to the question of how he managed to answer some of science's most perplexing riddles: Einstein said that most of his insights occurred when he was "playing with ideas."[41]

The virtues of play have not been lost on companies like Google, a company that famously incorporates playful décor and opportunities for play into its headquarters. Wikipedia's entry relates that "the lobby is decorated with a piano, lava lamps, old server clusters, and a projection of search queries on the wall. The hallways are full of exercise balls and bicycles . . . recreational amenities are scattered throughout the campus and include... assorted video games, foosball, a baby grand piano, a pool table, and ping pong."[42] Perhaps even more important for fostering creativity, Google staff are allowed to spend 20 percent of their work time on projects of their own choosing. Marissa Mayer, Google's Vice President of Search Products and User Experience, discovered that half of the new products Google launched were the result of experimentation and activities undertaken during that time set aside for personal creativity and experimentation.[43]

Despite the risks, library directors should encourage employees to play with the ideas that are fueling the digital explosion. When work becomes associated with play, employees are more at ease with each other, more relaxed, more productive, and may in fact make valuable "discoveries." Allowing staff to "play" at projects, or providing recreation time at work, might also result in improved creativity, improved morale, and harnessing the intelligence, originality, and capacity for problem solving of library staff. Additionally, a creative and playful environment might help attract talented and technically savvy staff to library work and help combat the image of libraries as dull and boring places, with rigid rules and stodgy staff.

# CONCLUSION

Search engines are marvels of technology and programming, yet—at least for the foreseeable future—they cannot completely unlock the treasures of libraries, especially treasures that are written in the full gamut of the world's languages, as well as treasures that might never be digitized. The library catalog and some form of cataloging, perhaps performed by "cyborg" or "bionic catalogers" who combine human judgment and machine processing, will be needed well into the future. But if catalogs and cataloging are to survive in any form, monumental changes will be needed. Will this be risky? Certainly, since risk of failure is always the flip side of change. But the risks associated with not changing are even greater. If catalogs and cataloging are lost, the entire library is at risk. In a 2008 column Roy Tennant described libraries as "hanging on for dear life," a situation that itself is not without considerable risk.[44]

How can the cataloging community find the way forward? Research is one avenue. The library profession needs evidence about what users want and need, evidence on which to build a road to the future. Additionally, Web 2.0 strategies can lead to entrepreneurially-inspired solutions. As Andy Budd stated, "Web 2.0 is not a thing, it's a state of mind."[45] It is with the goal of encouraging a participatory, collaborative, and entrepreneurial state of mind that Web 2.0 strategies should be explored, not so that libraries might jump mindlessly on the wiki or social tagging bandwagon or adopt technologies for their own sake, but so that librarians might thoughtfully glean lessons from these strategies, adapt them to their own ends, and fulfill the library profession's mission of preserving and providing access to the world's written record well into the future.

If catalog librarians take risks, they open themselves to the possibility of failure. However, if they do nothing, they marginalize themselves and the valuable work that they do. The risk of doing nothing far outweighs the risk of making changes to current practices.

## REFERENCE NOTES

1. For example, see Martha M. Yee, "Attempts to Deal with the Crisis in Cataloging at the Library of Congress in the 1940s," *Library Quarterly* 57, no. 1 (1987): 7 and Michael Gorman and Pat Oddy, *The Anglo-American Cataloging Rules Second Edition, Their History and Principles*, a paper for the International Conference on the Principles and Future Development of AACR, (Toronto, Ont.: Canadian Library Assn., 1998), 12.

2. Andrew Osborn, "The Crisis in Cataloging: A Shift in Thought Toward American Pragmatism," *Library Quarterly* 11, no. 4 (October 1941); Deanna B. Marcum, "*The Future of Cataloging*," address to the EBSCO Leadership Seminar, Boston, January 16,

2005, (Washington, D.C.: LC Professional Guild, 2005), www.guild2910.org/marcum. htm (accessed 7 January 2009).

3. Thomas Mann, *"On the Record," but Off the Track*, (Washington, D.C.: LC Professional Guild, 2008), 9, www.guild2910.org/WorkingGrpResponse2008.pdf (accessed 7 January 2009).

4. Tim O'Reilly, "What Is Web 2.0? Design Patterns and Business Models for the Next Generation of Software," *O'Reilly Radar* (September 30, 2005), www.oreillynet.com/pub/a/oreilly/tim/news/2005/09/30/what-is-web-20.html?page=1 (accessed 7 January 2009).

5. Ibid.

6. Tim O'Reilly, "Google Admits "Data is the Intel Inside," *O'Reilly Radar* (December 17, 2007), http://radar.oreilly.com/2007/12/google-admits-data-is-the-inte.html (accessed 7 January 2009).

7. John Reimer, "To Better Bibliographic Services: Expose, Expand, Extend Metadata Using Web 2.0," *NextSpace*, no. 2 (2006): 10, www.oclc.org/nextspace/002/5.htm (accessed 7 January 2009).

8. Resource, Description & Access: Constituency Review. Draft text Rule 1.7.1, www.rdaonline.org/constituencyreview/ (accessed 7 January 2009).

9. Miriam A. Drake, *Encyclopedia of Library and Information Science*, 2nd ed. (New York: Marcel Dekker, 2003): 2421.

10. Chris Anderson, "The Long Tail," *Wired* 12, no.10 (October 2004), www.wired.com/wired/archive/12.10/tail.html (accessed 7 January 2009).

11. "The Long Tail," *Wikipedia*, http://en.wikipedia.org/wiki/The_Long_Tail (accessed 7 January 2009).

12. Marcum, *On the Record*, 22.

13. Personal conversation between Diane Boehr and Dr. Lindberg at the NLM Board of Regents meeting, May 14, 2008.

14. O'Reilly, *What Is Web 2.0?* 4.

15. Marcum, *On the Record*, 37.

16. Marshall Keys, "Entrepreneurship and Risk in Libraries: Seizing and Creating Opportunities for Change," *Risk and Entrepreneurship in Libraries: Seizing Opportunities for Change*. (Chicago: ALA/ALCTS, 2009), 3.

17. O'Reilly, *What Is Web 2.0?* Sidebar: "West 2.0 Design Patterns," www.oreillynet.com/pub/a/oreilly/tim/news/2005/09/30/what-is-web-20.html (accessed 7 January 2009).

18. Owen Stephens, *Resource Discovery Infrastructure: What If We Were Starting from Scratch?* www.slideshare.net/ostephens/resource-discovery-infrastructure-what-if-we-were-starting-from-scratch-presentation (accessed 7 January 2009).

19. Marcum, *On the Record*, 11.

20. Linda K. Bartley and Regina R. Reynolds, "CONSER: Revolution and Evolution," *Cataloging & Classification Quarterly* 8, nos. 3–4 (1988): 53–55.

21. Roy Tennant, "The Future of Descriptive Enrichment," *LibraryJournal.com*, December 10, 2007, www.libraryjournal.com/blog/1090000309/post/1920018592.html (accessed 7 January 2009).

22. Marcum, *On the Record*, 24.

23. Kevin Kelly, "We Are the Web," *Wired,* 13 (August 2005), www.wired.com/wired/archive/13.08/tech.html (accessed 7 January 2009).

24. O'Reilly, *What Is Web 2.0?* Sidebar: "The Architecture of Participation," www.oreillynet.com/pub/a/oreilly/tim/news/2005/09/30/what-is-web-20.html?page=3 (accessed 7 January 2009).

25. Michael Arrington, "Encyclopedia Britannica now Free for Bloggers," *TechCrunch,* (April 18, 2008), www.techcrunch.com/2008/04/18/encyclopedia-britannica-now-free-for-bloggers/ (accessed 7 January 2009).

26. Karen Schneider, "The User Is Not Broken: A Meme Masquerading as a Manifesto," *Free Range Librarian,* (June 3, 2006), http://freerangelibrarian.com/2006/06/03/the-user-is-not-broken-a-meme-masquerading-as-a-manifesto/ (accessed 7 January 2009).

27. Suzanne Chapman, "Data: Students + Facebook + Library Outreach," *Userlib.com,* (15 December 2007), http://userslib.com/2007/12/15/data-students-facebook-library-outreach/ (accessed 3 February 2009).

28. Lynn Silipigni Connaway, "Mountains, Valleys, and Pathways: Serials Users' Needs and Steps to Meet Them. Part I: Identifying Serials Users' Needs: Preliminary Analysis of Focus Group and Semi-structured Interviews at Colleges and Universities," *Serials Librarian* 52, no. 1/2 (2007): 223–36, www.oclc.org/research/publications/archive/2007/connaway-serialslibrarian.pdf (accessed 7 January 2009).

29. Marcum, *On the Record,* 32.

30. Melissa L. Rethlefsen, "Tags Help Make Libraries Del.icio.us," *Library Journal.com,* (September 15, 2007), www.libraryjournal.com/article/CA6476403.html (accessed 7 January 2009).

31. "Barack Obama on Flickr," *Time,* (December 29, 2008), www.time.com/time/photogallery/0,29307,1866936,00.html (accessed on 7 January 2009).

32. "About Flickr," www.flickr.com/about (accessed 7 January 2009).

33. *For the Common Good: The Library of Congress Flickr Pilot Project,* www.loc.gov/rr/print/flickr_report_final.pdf (accessed 7 January 2009).

34. Josh Hadro, "Tagging Added to WorldCat.org," *Library Journal* (September 2008), www.libraryjournal.com/article/CA6600525.html (accessed 3 February 2009).

35. Ken Varnum, "New Tagging Tool at University of Michigan Library," *RSS4Lib,* (February 29, 2008), www.rss4lib.com/2008/02/new_tagging_tool_at_university.html (accessed 7 January 2009).

36. Roger von Oech, *A Whack on the Side of the Head* (New York: Warner Books, 1983), 86.

37. O'Reilly, *What Is Web 2.0?*

38. von Oech, *A Whack on the Side of the Head,* 74.

39. Bruce Copley, "Paradigm Paralysis: Causes, Complications and Cures," *Centre for Science Development Bulletin,* (March/April 1994), www.aahalearning.com/reading/room2/articles/Paradigm_Paralysis/#top (accessed 7 April 2009).

40. Dean Lucas, "Albert Einstein," *Famous Pictures, the Magazine,* (April 19, 2007), www.famouspictures.org/mag/index.php?title=Albert_Einstein (accessed 7 January 2009).

41. Lucas, "Albert Einstein."

42. "Google, Inc." *Wikipedia* http://en.wikipedia.org/wiki/Google (accessed 7 January 2009).

43. "Marissa Mayer's 9 Notions of Innovation," *Inspiration, Innovation,* June 16, 2006. Quoted in *EP//Experience Planner*, www.scottweisbrod.com/index.php/?p=90 (accessed 7 January 2009).

44. Tennant, "The Future of Descriptive Enrichment."

45. Andy Budd, *What Is Web 2.0?* (online presentation) www.andybudd.com/presentations/dcontruct05/ (accessed 7 January 2009).

# Two College Libraries Merge Their Technical Services Departments

## A Case Study of Denison University and Kenyon College

AMY BADERTSCHER and
LYNN SCOTT COCHRANE

While takeovers and mergers are common in the business world, they are less common in academe. It is certainly unusual for libraries, which are often deeply grounded in tradition, especially those at two different institutions, to consider merging their operations. However, in 2003, library staff at two independent Ohio academic institutions, Kenyon College and Denison University, broke with tradition and began to discuss the possibility of merging their technical services operations. Both wanted to expand their technical services functions to do a better job of managing digital resources without adding new staff. Since they already shared an online catalog, a daily delivery service, and a storage facility, they hoped that by merging their technical services operations they could achieve greater effectiveness and efficiency in routine, duplicative processes and thereby create time for exciting new activities related to next generation libraries. Neither library needed or wanted to downsize, but each was eager to utilize existing staff more effectively. Both library administrations knew that honesty and transparency about the motives for the project were mandatory—that was easy to say, because no staff would be eliminated, but it took more than a year before the staff really believed that they were not being asked to design themselves right out of a job. The good news is that the administrators were truthful about the reason for the changes and staff eventually believed and trusted them.

The conception and implementation of the merger, which began as an experiment, proved to be so successful that the two institutions signed a formal memorandum of understanding.

# BACKGROUND

Denison University and Kenyon College are liberal arts institutions located in small rural communities approximately 25 miles apart in Central Ohio. Libraries at the two schools have a long history of collaboration with various consortia, including the Five Colleges of Ohio and OhioLINK, a consortium of 89 academic and public libraries in Ohio.[1]

The Five Colleges of Ohio share in CONStor—a leased storage facility—participate in grant-funded initiatives for information literacy, and jointly license and acquire electronic resources. Four of the five institutions share a common integrated library system (ILS) known as CONSORT (Oberlin has its own ILS). All five schools also participate in cooperative collection development initiatives that relate to nonelectronic resources.

All OhioLINK member institutions participate in a statewide user-initiated borrowing program for books and other materials; cooperate in licensing more than 100 electronic databases, 6,000 electronic journals, and 40,000 electronic books; take advantage of statewide digital media collection initiatives; and collaborate on a statewide digital repository project.

Denison and Kenyon have a long history of institution-wide collaboration, due not only to their close geographic proximity, but also because the two schools have roughly comparable library collections, budgets, and staffing. See tables 1 and 2.

TABLE 1   Vital Statistics of the Two Schools, 2007–2008.

|  | DENISON UNIVERSITY | KENYON COLLEGE |
|---|---|---|
| Location | Granville, Ohio | Gambier, Ohio |
| Enrollment | 2,096 | 1,636 |
| Student/Faculty ratio | 10:1 | 10:1 |
| Total library expenditure | $3,093,015 | $3,010,436 |
| Total acquisitions budget | $1,213,878 | $1,219,767 |
| Total library staff FTE | 22.60 | 25 |
| Total technical services staff FTE | 5.75 | 5.5 |
| Total no. bound volumes | 460,349 | 436,000 |
| Total no. volumes added annually | 784* | 6,600 |
| No. print periodical subscriptions | 848 | 990 |

* Heavy weeding due to full stacks affected this number.

This table reflects the most current information and not necessarily the data submitted to CLIR.

## LAUNCHING THE PROJECT

In 2003, library leaders from Kenyon and Denison committed to under-taking a project to redesign technical services as part of a long-term com-mitment to ongoing cooperation. A grant from the Andrew W. Mellon Foundation provided support for the initial investigation and helped launch the project.

A task force consisting of two professional librarians and two parapro-fessionals from Denison, two librarians and three paraprofessionals from Kenyon, plus the CONSORT library system manager, was established and charged with preparing the grant proposal for a robust system for com-bined library technical services. The focus would be on creating a flex-ible, transferable, malleable, and adaptable organization positioned to meet constantly evolving patron information needs, research patterns, and desires for the Googlized world of scholarly resources.

The task force met weekly to define tasks and prepare a written frame-work for combining, or maintaining, separate operations. They reviewed the tasks involved and made decisions to maintain separate processes for time-sensitive tasks such as processing daily newspapers, or to take into account special interests and abilities of the staff. The task force identified critical infrastructure that would be necessary for full implementation of the plan and considered how to position the merged unit to be as innova-tive and forward-thinking as possible. Library directors from both schools consulted with the task force as needed but did not regularly attend meet-ings or direct the agenda. From the start, the process was staff-driven and designed to fulfill the charge and the principles established at the beginning of the initiative. Within three months, a grant proposal was finalized and submitted to the Mellon Foundation. Fortunately, the proposal was suc-cessful, as the resulting funding enabled the two libraries to effect change more quickly than would have been possible otherwise.

The team studied a number of critically important published works. They began by conducting their own environmental scan, which was heavily influ-enced by the richly detailed study *The 2003 OCLC Environmental Scan: Pattern Recognition*.[2] The second key influence on the work of the task force was *Reengineering the Corporation* by Michael Hammer and James Champy.[3] The new work was an expansion of Hammer's *Harvard Business Review* article that set the standard for corporate work redesign.[4] Though Hammer and Champy do not address higher education, or even libraries, the principles and examples in their book provided short-hand ways to describe what the project hoped to accomplish. A practical, library-based booklet by Jan Hayes and Maureen Sullivan, *Mapping the Process: Engaging Staff in Redesigning Work* provided a useful counterbalance to the corporate focus of Hammer and Champy.[5] Another work with direct applicability to the project was Mary McLaren's "Team Structure: Establishment and Evolution within Technical Services at the University of Kentucky Libraries," in *Library Collections, Acquisitions, and Technical Services* and Monteze Snyder's *Building Consensus: Conflict and Unity* was a useful team-building tool.[6] Finally, the most useful website the team consulted was Stanford University Libraries' *Technical Services Redesign Archive.*[7]

## KEY PLANNING PROCESSES

Rather than jumping immediately to the implementation phase, task force members took time to craft a vision statement and test and study the assumptions and principles they developed. A workflow model was created, followed by a plan for merging the two departments. Whenever the group drifted off track, someone would always remind the members of the group of the cliché, "if you don't know where you're going, you'll probably get there."[8] Developing the vision statement first and using it at every juncture helped the task force focus on the big picture, even as detailed procedures were being developed.

While the library directors and other campus leaders provided clear, patient, collaborative leadership, the success of the project also required:

- regular, transparent, and repeated communication of the broad goals and implications of the work to be done;
- constant reminders that the process, not the detailed tasks, are at issue;
- a thorough and well-reasoned proposal being in place before actual planning began;
- an experienced consultant to assist the project team with the difficult work of managing change.

To help guide its work, the task force hired two consultants to provide general oversight and training in group dynamics and provide the task force with detailed assessments of the technical services operations at both institutions.[9] Their input and direction were invaluable in creating the merger plan.

## DEVELOPING FOUNDATIONS FOR IMPLEMENTATION

Shared visions and goals were developed at the beginning of the project. Frequent meetings, discussion of the key readings, and celebration of every milestone created a true community of colleagues. Once that sense of community was achieved, it was sustained even when staff at either library retired or left, and it continued even as new staff were hired. Questioning the value of policies and procedures became the norm, and risk-taking was seen as desirable. The time and energy taken to build a solid team paid off handsomely. Both libraries were willing to commit significant staff resources to the project. For example, Kenyon redirected a vacant professional position to oversee the merged unit, while Denison committed substantial cataloging time to a multi-year government documents consolidation project.

## Creating Vision, Goal, and Objectives Statements

Establishing vision, goal, and objectives statements at the beginning of the process was critical to the success of the program. The following relatively simple statements, derived after lengthy and intense discussions, are included in the final report to the Mellon Foundation.[10] See figure 1.

---

### Vision Statement

Be Courageous!
>    Act as a collaborative unit to best serve users at multiple locations.
>    Provide intellectual representation of collection as a whole.
>    Foster a culture of staff empowerment that effectively utilizes and rewards individual strengths.
>    Enable research and development capacity for entire organization.
>    Appreciate that as we combine our processes, there may be activities best implemented separately.

### Goal

[To] improve access to information resources and create value-added services for our patrons through the cooperative efforts of the libraries of Denison University and Kenyon College.

### Objectives

[To] evaluate, plan, and implement a new model for providing collection management services to Denison University and Kenyon College. This will involve a complete examination of [library] processes from the time an item is identified for addition to the collections until it is placed on the shelf or is available to users electronically. This includes making information in all formats available to users.

(cont.)

---

FIGURE 1   Vision Statement for Merger.

FIGURE 1  Vision Statement for Merger. (cont.)

[To] reinvent library processes for handling physical objects and online resources.

[To] create a new technical services team for Denison and Kenyon. Key personnel from both schools will be included in the planning process. A Planning Task Force will secure input from all library personnel to reinvent existing workflows, integrate work processes for the two colleges, and create the team that will carry the work forward at the end of the grant period.

[To] move from manual authority control processing to machine-assisted processing provided by a vendor as an integral part of redesigning the work of the Technical Services departments. Machine-assisted processing provides accurate, efficient, and cost-effective loading of authority records to enrich our catalog and allows staff to work on other tasks, particularly those requiring intellectual activities.

[To] study, identify, and create new methods for providing access to [the] collections in addition to assessing and implementing shared processes for collection management. Access tools will recognize and incorporate the wide range of resources our constituents use. Managing and accessing electronic materials will be a central part of this redesign effort. Better oversight and management of [the] physical shared storage areas and . . . shared access tools, such as the CONSORT library catalog, will be achieved as well, . . . [creating] a culture by which this redesigned department will be proactive in anticipating changes in information delivery and searching mechanisms. The new team will be able to adapt work processes continually and thoughtfully by:

- Applying dramatic efficiencies to 80 percent of what is currently purchased and processed for the libraries.
- Streamlining receipt and delivery of materials.
- Reallocating resources to enhance the collections and collection access tools so they better serve constituents.
- Empowering staff to create and manage information in new and innovative ways for material in all formats.
- Enabling users to fully realize the liberal arts in an age of electronic information.

By a stroke of luck, during the evolution of the vision statement a document dating to 1994 was discovered that referred to plans by Denison, Kenyon, Ohio Wesleyan, and the College of Wooster to collaborate on the purchase of a shared integrated library system. At that time, Paul Gherman, then director of the library at Kenyon, wrote:

> the organizational restructuring of the four libraries was discussed to allow for the consolidating of technical services functions. Monographs could

be purchased and cataloged through a single monographic department for the four colleges. Serials might be acquired and processed through a single department. Standards for cataloging would need to be accepted by each of the four colleges, however, membership in OhioLINK would bring about this standardization.[11]

The sentiments expressed by Gherman made it clear that the concepts being developed in 2004 had already been envisioned a decade earlier.

## Planning Assumptions and Processes

The assumptions and principles articulated in figures 2 and 3, which were established for the planning processes, were critical to the ultimate success of both the grant and the creation of the merged technical services unit and they are referred to on a regular basis. The project:

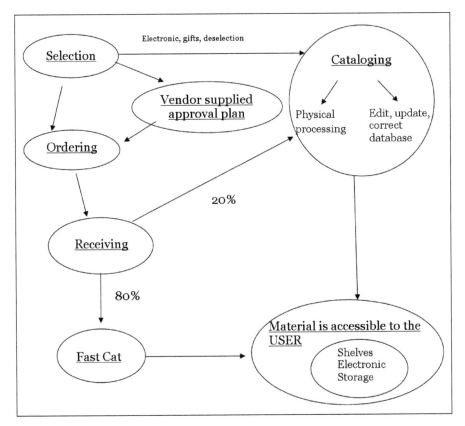

**FIGURE 2** Work Process Model.

Reproduced with the permission of the Council on Library and Information Resources.

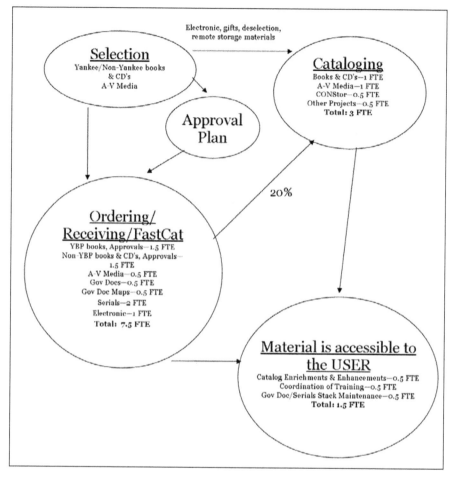

Electronic, gifts, deselection,
remote storage materials

**Selection**
Yankee/Non-Yankee books
& CD's
A-V Media

**Cataloging**
Books & CD's—1 FTE
A-V Media—1 FTE
CONStor—0.5 FTE
Other Projects—0.5 FTE
Total: 3 FTE

**Approval
Plan**

20%

**Ordering/
Receiving/FastCat**
YBP books, Approvals—1.5 FTE
Non-YBP books & CD's, Approvals—
1.5 FTE
A-V Media—0.5 FTE
Gov Docs—0.5 FTE
Gov Doc Maps—0.5 FTE
Serials—2 FTE
Electronic—1 FTE
Total: 7.5 FTE

**Material is accessible to
the USER**
Catalog Enrichments & Enhancements—0.5 FTE
Coordination of Training—0.5 FTE
Gov Doc/Serials Stack Maintenance—0.5 FTE
Total: 1.5 FTE

FIGURE 3   Staffing Model
Reproduced with the permission of the Council on Library and Information Resources.

- is designed with the needs of the users in mind;
- has the staff from Denison and Kenyon working as one unit to accomplish shared goals, thereby freeing time to devote to managing new formats;
- builds on the strengths of the staffs in the technical services areas;
- takes advantage of technology innovatively and productively to streamline work;
- creates a combined collection that is greater than the individual collections;

- adjusts to changes as necessary and will be transferable;
- focuses on the typical processes within the whole system;
- hinges on staff participation and empowerment to succeed.

Two additional factors influenced the work initially and they continue to influence the work in significant ways:

- whenever possible, workflows will be automated for the main stream of materials, and
- material will move between the two libraries as well as between the CONStor sites, for processing and for user access, with a turnaround time of no more than 24 hours.

Once the vision was defined and the assumptions outlined, the task force developed key processes and created a process map, a key work-activities map, a work process model, and a staffing model.

## IMPLEMENTING THE VISION

In early 2005, a three-member implementation team comprised of a librarian from Denison, a support staff member from Kenyon, and the joint system manager began fulfilling the plans and possibilities specified under the grant proposal of 2003. The workflows, previously outlined by the task force, were refined after a great deal of staff input.

The majority of staff time was devoted to monographic processing, therefore the first steps in the implementation of the joint technical services unit were the creation of a combined book acquisition and cataloging process, together with the introduction of a daily courier service between the two schools to supplement the one provided by OhioLINK. Combining the workflows from the two libraries was implemented in phases. Both libraries used Yankee Book Peddler (YBP) as their major book vendor, so YBP was the obvious choice as the vendor for the merged unit. Although YBP's online ordering system, GOBI, was implemented at both schools for collection development purposes, the actual ordering of all YBP materials began to be done by Denison staff, together with receiving and cataloging. The new merged unit took advantage of several YBP services, including electronic invoicing, the provision of shelf-ready materials, PromptCat profiling, the use of new property stamps, and the transference of older orders to GOBI. Mechanisms for quality control were also developed.

Arrangements were made for Kenyon to acquire and catalog all monographic materials obtained through sources other than YBP. Introduction

TABLE 2   Technical Services Staff Configuration at Denison and Kenyon, 2008

| NO. OF STAFF | DENISON | KENYON |
|---|---|---|
| Full-time | 5 | 4 |
| | supervisor/cataloger | manager/government documents specialist |
| | cataloger/special collections associate | monograph and music cataloger |
| | serials associate | acquisitions associate |
| | acquisitions associate | serials associate |
| | audio/video acquisitions/ cataloger | |
| Part-time | 2 | 2 |
| | government documents associates | acquisitions assistant |
| | | video cataloger |

of an electronic order form enabled fast and easy transmission of order requests by Denison staff to the staff at Kenyon. Non-YBP issues that were worked out included creating the online order form; initiating new and modifying old vendor accounts; training staff in invoicing and expanded uses of the ILS; developing a process for non-mainstream materials such as foreign language materials and items obtained from foreign publishers, music scores, and art works; and the identification of local cataloging practices. These tasks were detail-oriented and extremely time-consuming and involved a lot of trial-and-error as well as constant communication. Work imbalances between the two schools were inevitable and had to be accommodated.

## STAFFING

Denison and Kenyon have different structures for professional staff. Therefore, staffing recommendations for the merged library technical services unit focused on support staff positions.[12] They were asked to express interest in how they thought they might best contribute to the merged unit and their preferences were compared with the staffing allocation model and, when possible, job duties were assigned accordingly.

Based on the staffing model depicted in figures 2 and 3, processing teams were created for Ordering/Receiving/FastCat and Cataloging/User access.

**TABLE 3** Acquisition and Cataloging of Monographs, Audiovisuals, and Serials in the joint Denison-Kenyon Technical Services Unit.

| | DENISON | KENYON |
|---|---|---|
| **Monographs and standing orders** | | |
| Acquisitions | Orders all Yankee Book Peddler (YBP) materials for both Kenyon and Denison. YBP is the primary vendor. The majority of the materials from YPB are shelf-ready. | Orders all non-YBP materials and manages the majority of standing orders. |
| Cataloging | Catalogs all YBP materials for both Kenyon and Denison. | Catalogs all standing orders and non-YBP orders for both schools. These include out-of-print and foreign titles. |
| **Audiovisual materials** | | |
| Scores and CDs | Orders their own. Cataloged at Kenyon. | Orders and catalogs their own. |
| DVDs and videos | Orders and catalogs their own. Ordering and cataloging handled by the same individual. | Orders and catalogs their own. Ordering is done by one staff member and cataloged by another, part-time staff member. |
| **Serials** | | |
| Each school handles its own, but the associates are working together to streamline processes and examine ways to consolidate. | | |

The latter team focused on a variety of user access mechanisms for information resources, not solely the online catalog, but also included Google and other search engines. In addition, teams tied to material types were also defined for books/CDs/gifts, electronic resources/government documents/serials, and audiovisual media. Each support staff member was assigned to one processing team and one material type team.

In late 2005, Kenyon created the position of Associate Director (AD) of Collection Services to oversee the merged technical services unit. Denison staff participated fully in the search process, and the position was filled in February 2006. Initially the new supervisor was scheduled to work three days a week at Kenyon and two at Denison. This arrangement worked well and has been largely maintained to date. The AD's first step was to get to know the respective groups in order to learn what ideas the team had and where it was focusing its attention. Initially there were lingering doubts from staff regarding how the concept of a merged technical services unit would work in practice. Moreover technical services unit employees feared that the Associate Director had been hired as an "ax man." However, when it became clear that policies and practices would change but that no one's job was in jeopardy and that changes would be accompanied by expansive and free-flowing discussions, the staff relaxed, opened up, and began to share valuable ideas for improving and streamlining processes.

## MERGING

Having allayed staff fears and frustrations, the new supervisor faced the challenge of bringing the team closer together and helping members rethink their roles and goals. Social gatherings, frequent face-to-face meetings, and discussions by all members of the combined team helped with the reconceptualization effort.

Generating the motivation and momentum to keep the merger vibrant and fresh was another challenge for the staff. Despite the fact that the process redesign was at the forefront of everyone's mind, it was easy for staff to lapse back into a day-to-day task mentality. Keeping the final goal paramount has been and continues to be an ongoing challenge for the team as it reinvents roles and positions.

Significant strides have been made in enhancing skills and in taking advantage of talents of individual staff members. The introduction of PromptCat bibliographic records and the receipt of shelf ready material enabled staff to find the time to tackle backlogs of uncataloged materials and to work on other outstanding projects such as producing original cataloging records for a large collection of independently produced videos for which no OCLC records were available. Changes in workflow and the reallocation of staff resulted in more time for the cataloger to create original records and to make unusual materials visible and available to users.

## REFINING AND ADDING PROCESSES

The first year under the new Associate Director produced real progress as well as a few roadblocks. For example, all staff spent significant time reviewing the processes the two schools used to acquire and catalog audio-visual materials. Some of the conversations took place in person while others happened via video conferencing, a new technology that seemed appropriate to the topic. Kenyon indicated use of a modified Library of Congress classification scheme for music, while Denison applied accession numbers to the same kinds of materials. The reverse was true for videos and DVDs, where Denison used Library of Congress classification and Kenyon used accession numbers. After much debate about the merits of the methods and the issues that would be involved in changing these situations, it was decided that the methods employed at each school worked well for them at this time and should be maintained for the time being. While uniform treatment of the audiovisuals was rejected for the near term, it was decided that it would be beneficial to identify ways to improve the processing of these materials at some future time. The classification issue will almost certainly be revisited within a few years, as the two libraries reach for an appropriate level of standardization.

## SUSTAINING THE MERGED DEPARTMENT

In 2007, the libraries experienced a number of retirements, including Kenyon's Vice President of Library and Information Services, as well as Denison staff members with responsibility for serials and audio visual cataloging. These changes precipitated the movement to formalize the merger as well as provided a unique opportunity to review and evaluate staffing. First, to formalize the joint technical services unit, a memorandum of understanding between Kenyon and Denison was drafted and signed by the library directors and presidents of both institutions. The creation of the formal document recognizing the merger was a positive and important step and ensured that the program would continue and grow regardless of personnel changes.

At the same time, all current team members, plus staff from other library units in both libraries, participated in discussions about the needs of the joint technical services organization. It was quickly and easily decided that a full-time serials position should be maintained at Denison since the rapidly changing serials environment, with its influx of electronic resources, required at least one full-time position in serials at each institution. Serious and lengthy debate ensued, however, about the roles and responsibilities of the audio-visual cataloging position. As a result, the position was reconfigured to provide approximately half-time assistance to Denison's Special Collections, and Denison's DVD cataloging workload was transferred to the Denison staff member who handled audio-visual acquisitions. Because of the volume of work in audio-visual cataloging at the two schools, Kenyon continued to devote a part-time position to that function. Nevertheless, for the first time the merged unit could devote one full-time position to a complete workflow cycle. All staff saw this as a breakthrough development in work redesign.

The changes at Denison also created an opportunity at Kenyon when the acquisitions and cataloging workflow for music materials, including scores and CDs, was redesigned, thus providing an opportunity to recognize the talents of the cataloger whose primary interests were related to music. Ultimately, as a result of the reorganization, two staff members received not only additional responsibilities but ones that interested them both professionally and personally, creating a strong incentive to produce positive, even superior, results. The discussions surrounding the two Denison retirements highlighted the need for library managers to better understand not just the needs of the joint technical services unit but also of the talents and interests of the team members. Finding the best role for each individual was important to the success of the unit, and the reviews that ensued allowed the two libraries to leverage staff talents in the best possible areas.

At Kenyon, another retirement, this time in acquisitions, was announced in the fall of 2007 and although the retirement didn't occur because the retiree elected to remain in the position on a part-time basis, staff used the opportunity to review tasks and eliminate outdated procedures. Once again, a staffing change triggered a review of workloads and an examination of staff skills, talents and interests and gave staff the incentive to break away from traditional tasks that were no longer necessary.

The decision to merge technical services was so successful that staff in Denison's and Kenyon's government documents departments began to look at a collection consolidation project. Areas of overlap and duplication, as well as unique materials, were identified. Since the government documents committee within the Five Colleges of Ohio had long advocated collaboration, it quickly became apparent that the project would have an even greater impact if the four schools that shared an online catalog would pool their collective government document resources. Overtures were made to the College of Wooster and to Ohio Wesleyan University to participate in the government documents consolidation project, and the invitations were accepted. Now in its second year, this project has already generated a noticeable reduction in the overall size of the collection and has freed up considerable space in each library. Because government documents collections demand technical services staff time, the collaboration and cooperation had a ripple effect on technical services.

## CHALLENGES AND REACTIONS

The fifth year of the project, 2008, was in many ways a year of transition. Several successive institutional leadership changes and a decision not to refill (temporarily) two key positions at Kenyon created challenges in terms of library support. As a result, the role of the AD of Collection Services was expanded to include supervision of Kenyon's Special Collections and Circulation units.

Meanwhile, Denison experienced unexpected turnover when four out of eight librarians moved to other institutions in order to advance in their careers. This enormous changeover turned out to be beneficial for the technical services team because a librarian hired on a temporary basis was able to focus on electronic resources. The technical services group took advantage of the skills and knowledge of this individual to restructure the electronic resources workflow.

Inevitably, the personnel changes at Kenyon and Denison placed stress on their respective libraries, including the joint technical services group. The challenges were met by staff focusing on what was most important and, out of necessity, making changes from the bottom up. Streamlined workflows helped the staff achieve an acceptable level of contentment.

One of the objectives of the joint technical services team has been to thoroughly integrate the new employees into the work streams, to help them grow professionally and acquire the skills they need to be successful. In undertaking this work, it became clear that there was insufficient documentation for the dramatically different roles and responsibilities that had evolved for the technical services staff. It was equally obvious that the effects of ongoing technological adaptations are also playing a major role in the staff's development. Therefore, the group made the decision to revise and expand documentation and to prepare plans regarding backup coverage during absences.

A backup plan was created for each member of the joint technical services team. The objective was to identify not only logical, suitable substitutes who could cover from 75 to 80 percent of the day-to-day work but also to identify work that absolutely had to be accomplished as well as tasks that could be postponed. In many cases the most suitable backup for each task was located at the other library. During this exercise, the need for more than one person in the joint unit to be familiar with all tasks became glaringly obvious. It was also clear that the two institutions needed to work out a standard form of notification for absences.

Throughout the work redesign process, serials management presented challenges for Denison and Kenyon. This was particularly felt during major cancellations of print journals which occurred at both institutions when full-text electronic journals replaced print. Although the cancellation projects are very labor intensive and require a high level of knowledge and expertise, the reductions are financially justified and the cancellation of print decreases the strain on already overcrowded shelves, lowers bindery costs, and gives the libraries an opportunity to consider other consolidation possibilities. Most important, the users much prefer full-text electronic journals over print.

Staff involved in serials management at Kenyon and Denison have initiated quarterly in-person discussions with members of the serials staff at the other two CONSORT libraries to talk about serials issues in general, cancellation scenarios, and digital access to electronic resources. Once again, cooperation should help elicit change from the bottom-up and future consolidation or redesign plans may well emerge from these discussions.

## WHAT WORKED AND WHAT DID NOT

The lessons Kenyon and Denison learned from the shared journey was just as important as the ultimate goal of creating a more effective and efficient technical processing operation. Trust was built among all staff in the two libraries. Commitment and involvement at all levels—from top administrators to part-time support staff—were instrumental in developing a successful grant proposal and following through with the creation of a merged department. Once trust was established, building the team comprised of existing staff members who had every reason to be suspicious worked surprisingly well.

Later, new staff were hired with the clear understanding that the merged department functions as a team and that travel between locations may be necessary. In fact, the staff embraced this concept and, although reasons to travel are rare, they are occasionally necessary, mainly to deal with processing of collections outside the mainstream that require special attention. Being able to take advantage of technology, plus the daily courier service between the two libraries, facilitates the ability of staff to work together as a team despite the physical distance that separates them.

In almost every case, what did not work can be attributed to lapses in communication or communication difficulties. Keeping everyone in the loop with regard to both major and minor decisions has been challenging. The libraries experimented with various methods for sharing information including e-mail, Google Docs, and message boards, but no single solution has proven to be very effective.

Since both libraries were thriving and users were satisfied, it was sometimes difficult for administrators to articulate convincingly the need for the merger. In addition, it took the staff in each library a long time to begin to let go of what they felt were home-grown "perfect" processes and procedures and to accept mutually acceptable "good enough" substitutes instead. However, once the mind-set of the staff changed, they were able to see that there was sufficient time to take on additional—often interesting and exciting—new projects. Eventually, the transition was almost universally accepted.

## SUMMARY

Integrating the two technical services units continues to be a work in progress, and goals for the future are as follows:

- evaluate all job descriptions and request upgrades or changes with the respective human resources departments;
- create documentation for all functions to support backup and cross-training;
- increase training and professional development for staff to continue to expand the potential of the organization;
- continue to review and change the "Ken/Den project" so that it remains fresh and interesting;
- continue to seek ways to streamline workflow and work processes;
- seek better methods of collaborating and communicating within the joint organization;
- implement a shared classification method for all audio-visual material;
- move toward using a single binder with a combined shipping plan to reduce costs and time spent on the bindery process;
- reduce the number of paper periodicals and create a shared collection from the remaining titles.

Work redesign in library technical services required input and support from two separate institutions, two administrations, and the involvement of many staff. The project, while challenging, has shown tangible and positive results. It has been difficult to measure the changes quantitatively but qualitative measures are evident. For example, now there is time to undertake and complete special projects, eliminate backlogs, and perform original cataloging. In addition, many of the electronic tools used on a daily basis are more efficient than in the past and make it possible to modify or reduce paper workflows. The original organizational model in place at each institution was not conducive to accomplishments of this nature. A new organizational model was required before relevant changes could be realized.

One of the most critical challenges facing libraries is to continue to enhance services and provide opportunities for staff to enhance their skills. Library administrators must encourage professional development and risk taking in order to compete and remain relevant in the emerging global electronic information environment. The best ideas for improving workflows and services often come from the staff handling day-to-day operations on the front lines. All staff must be encouraged to think critically about the details of the work they are doing, the steps needed to accomplish a task, and what parts of the task add value to the process. When staff are encouraged to participate in the process, the modification or even elimination of tasks can be accomplished. Kenyon and Denison will continue to encourage staff participation in conferences and training programs so they can enhance and expand their overall knowledge and skills. In addition, opportunities to meet with colleagues in other libraries who are working on the same or similar issues are encouraged.

The knowledgebase of workers entering the academic library market as paraprofessionals is different today than it was twenty or thirty years ago. Academic libraries need to expand the conceptual basis of these positions into more well-rounded roles within the organization—the days of defining library paraprofessionals as "mere" clerical staff are over. Kenyon and Denison are focused on rethinking the roles of technical services staff and redefining positions. For example, the roles for cataloging and acquisitions staff can and will be more dynamic and creative than they have been traditionally, in part due to automation and the possible elimination of many routine functions. Academic libraries will need to adjust not only the relevant position descriptions, but also the salary ranges for these roles. The terms "support staff" and "paraprofessional" are evolving. Perhaps new descriptors will be developed that will provide both internal and external audiences with a better sense of what technical services work involves and what kinds of knowledge, skills, and abilities are required for organizational success.

Technical services are evolving, and the next generation of technical services positions will be different from those in place today. Technology makes it possible to expand the number and variety of scholarly information resources and thereby offers opportunities for creativity and innovation in how our libraries serve users. While many librarians will view the merger scenario described here as risky, the Kenyon-Denison combined technical services department has created a flexible, adaptable organization capable of handling the challenges of the future.

## REFERENCE NOTES

1. Five Colleges of Ohio: Denison University, Kenyon College, the College of Wooster, Oberlin College, and Ohio Wesleyan University.
2. Cathy DeRosa, *The 2003 OCLC Environmental Scan: Pattern Recognition*, (Dublin, Ohio: OCLC, 2004).
3. Michael Hammer and James Champy, *Reengineering the Corporation*, (New York: Harper Collins, 2001).

4. Michael Hammer, "Re-engineering Work: Don't Automate, Obliterate," *Harvard Business Review* 68, no. 4 (July/August 1990): 104–12.

5. Jan Hayes and Maureen Sullivan, *Mapping the Process: Engaging Staff in Redesigning Work,* (Wheeling, Ill.: North Suburban Library System, 2002).

6. Mary McLaren, "Team Structure: Establishment and Evolution within Technical Services at the University of Kentucky Libraries," *Library Collections, Acquisitions, and Technical Services,* 25 (Winter 2001): 357–69 and Monteze Snyder, *Building Consensus: Conflict and Unity,* (Richmond, Ind.: Earlham Press, 2001).

7. Stanford University Libraries, *Technical Services Redesign Archive,* http://library.stanford .edu/depts/ts/about/redesign/ (accessed 3 February 2009)

8. Similar phrases have been attributed to Confucius and to Lewis Carroll.

9. Maureen Sullivan (http://maureensullivan.org/) and R2 Consulting (www.ebookmap .net/).

10. Internal document from Denison/Kenyon to the Mellon Foundation, December 23, 2005. See also Debra K. Andreadis, et al., *Cooperative Work Redesign in Library Technical Services at Denison University and Kenyon College,* (Washington, D.C.: Council on Library and Information Resources, 2007), www.clir.org/pubs/reports/pub139/ denken.html (accessed 9 February 2009).

11. Minutes of the Five Colleges of Ohio library directors' meeting, May 25, 1994.

12. Kenyon professionals are called Library Technology Consultants because they cover both library and desktop technology support. Denison's professionals follow the traditional model of librarians with technology support handled by the Information Technology Services department on campus.

## BIBLIOGRAPHY

Andreadis, Debra, Christopher D. Barth, Lynn Scott Cochrane, and Karen E. Greever. "Cooperative Work Redesign in Library Technical Services at Denison University and Kenyon College," in *Library Workflow Redesign: Six Case Studies*, ed. by Marilyn Mitchell. Washington, D.C.: Council on Library and Information Resources, 2007, 39–49

Chase, Anne and Tony Krug. "New Techniques in Library Technical Services at the Appalachian College Association." *Library Workflow Redesign: Six Case Studies*, ed. by Marilyn Mitchell. Washington, D.C.: Council on Library and Information Resources, 2007, 8–20.

DeRosa, Cathy, Lorcan Dempsey and Alane Wilson. *The 2003 OCLC Environmental Scan: Pattern Recognition.* Dublin, Ohio: OCLC, 2004.

Gunter, Linda and Cindy Snyder. "Reference and Information Services Redesign at The Libraries of The Claremont Colleges." *Library Workflow Redesign: Six Case Studies*, ed. by Marilyn Mitchell. Washington, D.C.: Council on Library and Information Resources, 2007, 21–38.

Hammer, Michael and James Champy. *Reengineering the Corporation: A Manifesto for Business Revolution.* New York: Harper Collins, 2001.

Hayes, Jan, Maureen Sullivan and Amy Bernath. *Mapping the Process: Engaging Staff in Redesigning Work.* Wheeling, Ill.: North Suburban Library System, 2002.

Loring, Christopher B. "Increasing Productivity through Workflow Redesign at Smith College." *Library Workflow Redesign: Six Case Studies*, ed. by Marilyn Mitchell. Washington, D.C.: Council on Library and Information Resources, 2007, 50–59.

McLaren, Mary. "Team Structure: Establishment and Evolution within Technical Services at the University of Kentucky Libraries." *Library Collections, Acquisitions, and Technical Services*. 25, no. 4 (Winter 2001): 357–69.

Medeiros, Norm. "Managing Electronic Resources in the Tri-College Consortium." *Library Workflow Redesign: Six Case Studies*, ed. by Marilyn Mitchell. Washington, D.C.: Council on Library and Information Resources, 2007, 60–72.

Mitchell, Marilyn, ed. *Library Workflow Redesign: Six Case Studies*. Washington, D.C.: Council on Library and Information Resources, 2007. www.clir.org/pubs/reports/ pub139/pub139.pdf (accessed 6 June 2009).

Mitchell, Marilyn. "Library Workflow Redesign: Concepts and Results." in *Library Workflow Redesign: Six Case Studies*, ed. by Marilyn Mitchell. Washington, D.C.: Council on Library and Information Resources, 2007, 1–7.

Parham, Loretta and Carolyn Hart. "Redesigning Services at The Robert W. Woodruff Library of the Atlanta University Center, Inc." *Library Workflow Redesign: Six Case Studies*, ed. by Marilyn Mitchell. Washington, D.C.: Council on Library and Information Resources, 2007, 73–81.

Snyder, Monteze M, Cheryl Gibbs, Susan A. Hillman, Trayce N. Peterson, Joanna Schofield, and George Watson. *Building Consensus: Conflict and Unity*. Richmond, Ind.: Earlham Press, 2001.

"Technical Services Redesign Archive." *Stanford University Libraries*. 7 May 2004. www .sul.stanford.edu/depts/ts/about/redesign/ (accessed Dec. 13, 2008).

# McMaster University Libraries 2.0

*Transforming Traditional Organizations*

JEFFREY G. TRZECIAK

ibraries today are at the heart of a major transformation on university campuses. Fueled by emerging technologies, changing student and faculty expectations and use patterns, changing teaching strategies, and evolving digital scholarship, libraries have changed dramatically as well. No longer book warehouses, libraries have become centers for teaching, learning, and research.

While these changes have had a profound impact on libraries and library services, the traditional library strength of connecting people to information is still relevant today. In fact, it can be said that twenty-first-century fluencies (information fluency, numeracy, visual fluency, media fluency, scientific fluency, and geospatial fluency) are essential elements to a quality education in our flattened world. In order to be successful post-graduation, students must possess the skills necessary to access and use information, regardless of format, efficiently, effectively, legally, and ethically.

Over the past two years, the McMaster University Libraries have undertaken a dramatic transformation from a very traditional academic library to an innovative, user-centered partner in teaching, learning, and research. It is an evolution that culminated in the receipt of the 2008 Association of College and Research Libraries (ACRL) Excellence in Academic Libraries award, which was bestowed in recognition of "a successful transformation from a traditional research library to an innovative, user-centered library using technological advances to accomplish its goals."[1]

Successful organizations are measured, in part, by their ability to adapt to the changing needs and expectations of their users. Adaptation requires a culture of risk-taking and innovation that encourages and rewards the radical rethinking of library resources and services. The McMaster University community is recognized for its ability to lead by reinterpreting and reinventing itself. The appointment of a new university librarian and the hiring of eight new librarians provided the library with an opportunity to make some significant organizational changes to meet the needs of academic library users in the twenty-first century.

Aademic libraries interested in organizational transformation can use this example to gain insight into the changed library as it progressed from traditional to innovative. While many of the examples represent common themes in academic libraries, the McMaster approach is unique because the changes were accomplished over a brief, two-year period of time. McMaster's success can be used as a model for other institutions interested in thoughtful and rapid transformational change.

## McMASTER UNIVERSITY

Founded in 1887, McMaster University is located in Hamilton, Ontario, Canada. The university supports more than 20,000 full time students, representing a significant increase in enrollment in the last decade. More than 1,400 full-time faculty can be found in the faculties of health sciences, engineering, science, business, humanities, and social sciences.

As an early pioneer of problem-based learning, McMaster has a long-standing reputation as Canada's most innovative university and typically ranks at or near the top in research intensity among Canadian universities. According to a ranking prepared by Shanghai Jiao Tong University, McMaster now ranks as one of the top hundred universities in the world.[2] The university's vision is "to achieve international distinction for creativity, innovation and excellence."[3] Given McMaster's reputation, it follows that it should have a library with an equally impressive reputation for innovation and excellence.

## McMASTER UNIVERSITY LIBRARIES

The McMaster University Libraries consist of the Mills Memorial Library (humanities and social sciences), Innis Library (business), H. G. Thode Library of Science and Engineering, and the Health Sciences Library. The four libraries opened their doors in 1951, 1974, 1978 and 1971 respectively and today are easily among the busiest buildings on campus, achieving a combined gate count of almost 2.5 million visitors annually.

The collections of the libraries total more than 2 million books, 20,000 print and electronic journal titles, and an additional 200,000 e-resources. General collection strengths support the research and teaching strengths of the university with particular emphasis on biology, British history, business, chemistry, classics, economics, engineering, English literature, geography and earth sciences, health sciences, maps, nuclear physics, and religious studies. The William Ready Division of Archives and Research Collections houses extensive archives including those of Bertrand Russell, a noteworthy collection of eighteenth-century literature, and extensive materials related to the two world wars.

As a large academic library, McMaster is a member of several organizations including the Association of Research Libraries (ARL), the Canadian Association of Research Libraries (CARL), the Coalition for Networked Information (CNI), and the Center for Research Libraries (CRL).

At the beginning of the twenty-first-century, the library was in decline and faced a number of significant challenges. In response, in 2002, the provost formed an ad-hoc committee with broad representation and chaired by a member of the faculty, to identify the key challenges facing the library and to make recommendations to address them. The committee identified three areas of concern:

*congruence*—an absence of relationships between academic and curriculum planning campus-wide and the libraries;

*governance*—a disconnect between library operations and the academic community's needs; and

*vision*—an absence of leadership and long-range view to challenge the university community to think about the library of the future.

By 2006 a search for a new university librarian had been completed and the library transformation had been launched.

## McMASTER UNIVERSITY LIBRARY 2.0: PREPARING FOR THE TRANSFORMATION

The McMaster University community is recognized for its ability to reinterpret and reinvent itself based on long-standing traditions of creative thinking and innovation. In 2006, the library launched its plans for transformation. Because the library had no formal role on any of the university's major governing bodies, it was critical that the library adopt a stance that would allow it to reposition itself as a leader on campus. The library also needed to engage the campus community in a meaningful discussion about its current and possible future needs. To set the stage, a 2.0 mentality of flexibility, risk-taking, and experimentation called "Library 2.0 @ Mac" was embraced.

A transformation team, appointed by the university librarian, worked for three months to develop a new transformative model directly aligned with the academic faculties and the strategic directions of the university. The team worked with consultants on a stakeholder review; invited internationally recognized leaders in librarianship to discuss trends in academia; and met with library staff individually and in groups to get input into the process. A series of guest speakers were invited to give talks to library staff in areas of emerging interest: Michael Stephens, Instructor in the Graduate School of Library and Information Science at Dominican University, presented "Web 2.0"; Perry Willett, the Head of Digital Library Production Service at the University of Michigan, spoke about Google's digitization projects; Michael Ridley, Chief Librarian at the University of Guelph, discussed the future of libraries; Joan Lippincott, Associate Executive Director of the Coalition for Networked Information, familiarized staff with "The Net Generation"; and Carla Stoffle, Dean of Libraries and Center for Creative Photography at the University of Arizona, delivered a talk about "Organizational Transformation."

The team also conducted an extensive organizational review with the assistance of an external consultant. Their report became the basis for an organizational transformation focused broadly on four areas:

- transforming ourselves;
- transforming our spaces;
- transforming our services;
- transforming our resources.

While significant changes in services and resources took place as part of the library's transformation, the focus of this chapter is on the transformation of the staff and facilities.

## IMPLEMENTING THE TRANSFORMATION

Recognizing that staff is the library's number-one resource, a process of reorganization was initiated that was intended to accomplish four goals:

- streamline or outsource tasks that do not add value for users;
- reallocate positions to new services and new priorities based on user needs and changing expectations;

- provide training and development opportunities for staff to position them to assume new responsibilities; and
- more closely integrate the libraries with the academic departments across campus.

A key component to the process of staff transformation was renewal. Working collaboratively with the union and university human resources, the library offered an early retirement incentive to all eligible staff members; sixteen individuals took advantage of that offer. Those early retirements made it possible to dramatically streamline back-office processes such as cataloging, and to automate others, such as checkout. They also facilitated the elimination of departments such as copy cataloging, and the merging of others such as circulation and inter-library loan. Emphasis was placed on public services, with some staff, including former full-time catalogers, assuming new roles in public services to provide support for instant messaging (IM) and for Second Life research. Additionally, the creation of new middle-management positions provided opportunities for the staff to advance and eased the workload for the supervisors of newly merged service areas such as circulation, research help, and inter-library loan.[4] The vacancies created by the early retirement program resulted in the creation of 8 new professional positions:

*Immersive Learning/Gaming Librarian.* To develop and deploy new technologies such as gaming and virtual worlds to make libraries relevant to today's tech-savvy students;

*Digital Technologies Development Librarian.* To manage the transition from a commercial integrated library system to Evergreen, the enterprise-class open source library automation system;[5]

*Digital Strategies Librarian.* To manage digital initiatives, providing vision and leadership in the development of a library digitization strategy;

*Marketing, Communications and Outreach Librarian.* To develop and implement a marketing and communications program for the library, increasing the library's profile both on and off-campus;

*Teaching and Learning Librarian.* To provide leadership in integrating the library into the teaching and learning mission of the university;

*E-Resources Librarian.* To provide leadership in identifying new electronic information resources and coordinating their evaluation and purchase;

*Archivist/Librarian.* To work with the Director of Research Collections in building and promoting the library's world-class special collections; and

*Data/GIS Librarian.* To work with the campus community to promote and provide support for the use of data/Geographic Information System technology in the library.

The restructuring allowed the library to place greater emphasis on public service, particularly the user experience, and to increase its emphasis on development of digital resources, integrate the libraries into teaching/learning, participate in new collaborative initiatives with other area academic libraries, and provide leadership in a growing area of interest—immersive learning environments. In summary, the library moved from a model of transaction-based services to one of pedagogy and learning services.

Even with the early retirements and new hires, it was clear that success would only be possible with additional staff training and development. In order to identify staff development needs and share information among staff about professional development activities and job-related training opportunities, the library created a needs-assessment survey and a staff development and training web site. Staff members were asked to identify the types of professional development they would find most useful and, since different people have different learning styles, indicate the learning model that would best suit their needs.

In early 2007, the library staff participated in Learning 2.0 @ Mac, a hands-on, immersive learning program that provided an opportunity to explore Web 2.0 tools and discover the impact these tools are having on libraries and library services.[6] The program was self-directed, low-threat, and above all, fun. Eighty-four library staff members voluntarily enrolled in the program. Each week, participants focused on a particular technology and were given a task that would entice them to practice their new skills using freely available online tools such as Blogger, WordPress, Bloglines, del.icio.us, and Facebook. Sixty-eight members of the library staff, or a little more than 50 percent, completed the program along with some staff from University Advancement who also participated in the weekly activities.

## TRANSFORMING THE SPACES

Recognizing that the library may be the most important observation post for studying how students really learn, the space transformations have had one goal: to transform the libraries into Canada's most innovative space dedicated to learning.[7] In order to realize that goal, the library faced a number of challenges, including many common to most academic libraries:

- demand for increased study space coupled with declining use of physical collections;
- rising enrollment combined with rising gate counts at the library;
- changing student expectations for a range of study spaces (silent and collaborative); and
- increased pressure from the university administration to provide space in the library for other academic departments and functions.

In order to address these challenges, several physical renovation projects were undertaken, including a major redesign of a traditional library reading room into the Mills Learning Commons. Armed with information from a concept feasibility study, a series of public consultations, and a thorough examination of the learning commons model at other institutions, approximately 7,000 square feet of library space was renovated to become the Mills Learning Commons.[8] Once a drab and outdated reading room with none of the high-tech functionality required by library users today, the Mills Learning Commons is now an active and student-centered learning space. It integrates traditional and emerging scholarly resources with information technology and offers expert help and instruction with work spaces for both collaborative and individual study. The result is open, ergonomic, computing spaces; lounge spaces with soft seating (chosen by students via a "vote with your seat" contest); collaborative study rooms; bookable consultation rooms; and new spaces for academic skills counseling, services to students with disabilities, and expert IT help. One hundred and seventy state-of-the-art computers, full wireless access, new printers and scanners, productivity software and special software for students with disabilities were also added.

Based on the success with the Mills Learning Commons, a second learning commons project for the H. G. Thode Library of Science and Engineering was launched.[9] The project will create a high-tech/high-touch facility that is attractive to students and faculty alike. It is intended as a space that changes attitudes, practice, and outcomes. Students and faculty will have access to high-end computing workstations, multimedia pods, wireless networking, and laptops. There will be welcoming spaces for individual study and quiet reflection as well as enhanced places for research and IT assistance. Small group study areas featuring interactive whiteboards and plasma displays plus classrooms and breakout rooms enabled with video conferencing, podcasting, and podcasting equipment will be created as well as collaboration spaces for faculty and graduate students to work on their teaching. The Commons will also serve as the future home for the Faculty of Science's integrated Honours Science program (iSci).

## LIBRARY SYSTEMS

A number of less tangible renovations were also initiated that have radically transformed the virtual learning environment, beginning with the integrated library system and the online library catalog. By selecting Endeca's *Information Access Platform* as the library's discovery layer, McMaster became the first Canadian library to implement faceted browsing.[10] The transformation of the catalog was significant. No longer required to wade through a first-in/first-out catalog, students and faculty can easily locate the materials they need. Search results can be quickly ranked by relevance, and navigation topics refined by author, genre, language, and material type. As users increasingly turn to electronic resources as their primary source for information, this easy-to-use approach has reinvigorated interest in both print and electronic library collections.

Building on the success of the catalog transformation, the library has now undertaken a project to replace the integrated library system itself with Evergreen, the open source system. Together with the University of Windsor, Laurentian University, and Algoma College, the library established Conifer (http://conifer.mcmaster.ca), a collaborative project to develop a shared instance of Evergreen. Unlike traditional commercial systems, the open source product Evergreen will allow the libraries to manage collection resources more efficiently and respond more rapidly to changing user needs.

## WEB 2.0

In the winter of 2007, the McMaster libraries began to expand their traditional support services to include hosting blogs and wikis for faculty members interested in using these tools for teaching and research. The 2.0 toolbox (http://blog.lib.mcmaster.ca/) can be used to extend in-class discussions, promote group work, and provide a platform for collaboration and distributed research in a noncommercial and ad-free academic environment. A few examples of projects include:

> The Geography and Earth Sciences Liaison Librarian collaborated with two professors on wiki assignments for a fourth-year geography class on the changing Canadian glacial landscape and a third-year class on segregation in world cities. Charged with the task of gathering and organizing large quantities of information, students

produced results that far exceeded expectations. They collaborated to solve problems and meet challenges, using the wiki format to creative advantage and experiencing firsthand the satisfaction of seeing their results accessible on the Internet. The fact that the assignment was to be graded seemed to be forgotten as the teams fed off each other's ideas and critically engaged with the topic.

The Mac Library Experience wiki (http://libfye.wetpaint.com/?t=anon) is a one-stop shop, providing essential information about the library for new students. The wiki format allows students to post and share tips and advice and post comments. One unique feature of the Mac Library Experience wiki is a calendar of events, including introductory tours of all four campus libraries and workshops designed to help students achieve academic success.

McMaster's Map Collection (http://library.mcmaster.ca/maps/air photos/1919.htm) uses a Google Maps mashup as an index for a heavily used collection of 5,000 local aerial photos. This tool allows researchers to zoom to their research site using Google Maps and then see whether McMaster Library has photos covering that site for any period since 1919. The convenience of this website has eliminated the need for users to make a special trip to the library to consult paper indexes.

## WEB 3.0

In collaboration with the Hamilton Public Library and Mohawk College, the library is moving from Web 2.0 to Web 3.0, by investing in the development of a space in Second Life with the recent purchase of an island.[11] The island will position the library as a leader in the exploration of library services, collections, and spaces in the virtual world. It will consist of space for both large and small group collaboration and instruction and include an area for experimentation and discovery and room for 3D exhibits of the library's digital resources, as well as services such as reference assistance and instruction. For example, the island is home to a class project for students in a Multimedia Digital Games course in which a sculpture garden was created as a result of a collaborative class project between the faculty, the libraries, and the students.

## NEXT STEPS

After so much change in less than 24 months, it seemed appropriate to step back and take another look at the direction that had been charted for the libraries. That included a series of half-day retreats with all library staff where groups brainstormed and developed model vision and mission statements and outlined values and strategic directions. The comments from those sessions were then consolidated and clarified by the senior management team with the assistance of an outside consultant.[12] The result was a new strategic plan that redefines the library's vision, mission and goals and ensures that they align with the University's reputation for innovation and academic excellence. The high level of staff involvement in the planning process resulted in a greater degree of ownership for the plan and the strategic goals. The vision statement—"McMaster University Library will be recognized as Canada's most innovative, user-centred, academic library"—expresses the library's aspirations.[13] The mission statement

> "The University Library advances teaching, learning and research at McMaster by:
>
> - teaching students to be successful, ethical information seekers
> - facilitating access to information resources
> - providing welcoming spaces for intellectual discovery
> - promoting the innovative adoption of emerging learning technologies"

is explicit about the library's role as the hub of the institution's intellectual life. A set of core values outline what will be needed to realize the vision and mission:

- excellent customer service
- collaboration, innovation, creativity and risk taking
- inclusiveness and respect for the individual
- accountability for our actions and decisions

## CONCLUSION

Above all, the experience of the last several years has taught the staff of the McMaster libraries not to be afraid of change. It is imperative for librarians at all levels to be involved in and to provide leadership for change that extends beyond the library's walls and beyond its traditional roles. In order for the library to grow and flourish as an organization, librarians must have an understanding of current issues and, as catalysts for change, they must go beyond simply reacting to or embracing these issues. In order to redefine the profession, it is crucial that librarians open their minds to new ideas, forge new partnerships and look to the future rather than the past.

## REFERENCE NOTES

1. *ACRL Excellence in Academic Libraries Winners Announced*, January 29, 2008, www .ala.org/ala/newspresscenter/news/pressreleases2008/january2008/academic08.cfm (accessed 3 January 2009).

2. Shanghai Jiao Tong University, *2008 Academic Rankings of World Universities*. www .arwu.org/rank2008/ARWU2008_A(EN).htm (accessed 12 February 2009).

3. McMaster University Office of Public Relations, *Mission and Vision: Inspiring Innovation & Discovery*, www.mcmaster.ca/opr/html/opr/fast_facts/main/mission.html (accessed 3 January 2009).

4. The Transformed McMaster University Library System, http://library.mcmaster.ca./about/orgchart.pdf (accessed 13 February 2009).

5. Evergreen, http://evergreen-ils.org/ (accessed 12 January 2009).

6. A. Etches-Johnson, *About Learning 2.0 @ Mac*, http://macetg.wordpress.com/about -learning-20-mac/ (accessed 3 January 2009).

7. J. Duderstadt, William A. Wulf, Robert Zemsky, "Envisioning a Transformed University," *Issues Online in Science and Technology* (Fall 2005), www.issues.org/22.1/ duderstadt.html (accessed 3 January 2009).

8. Mills Learning Center, http://library.mcmaster.ca/mission/learning-commons (accessed 12 January 2009).

9. Thode Renovation blog, http://thodereno.blog.lib.mcmaster.ca/ (accessed 12 January 2009).

10. Endeca's *Information Access Platform*, http://endeca.com/technology/index.html (accessed 10 January 2009).

11. SLurl: Location-based linking in Second Life, http://slurl.com/secondlife/Steel%20 City/128/128/0 (accessed 12 January 2009).

12. McMaster University Libraries, Mission, Planning Documents and Reports, http:// library.mcmaster.ca/about/mission.htm (accessed 12 January 2009).

13. Ibid.

# Warning: When Rowing Forward This Boat May Rock!

RIVKAH SASS

Despite being smart people, librarians have allowed others to develop solutions and set agendas for them that do not work. Moreover, they have not been proactive about creating the future of libraries and have not taken advantage of tools that would make a difference for users. The result, while perhaps not extinction, is the very real possibility that libraries will be increasingly marginalized. In order to retool themselves and to thrive, librarians need to take lessons from entrepreneurs, the creative class, and from one another. They must not be afraid to use proven strategies from other disciplines. They must develop their own brand while developing strategic partnerships that extend their reach. This means fostering a climate that is conducive to risk-taking and is sensitive to human considerations. All staff members must be encouraged to embrace entrepreneurial opportunities and be allowed to participate in discussions with in-house staff, potential external partners, and users about what it means to be a twenty-first century library.

## LOSING THE INFORMATION BATTLE

For more than thirty years, the online systems and processes used by libraries have been more about control than access. This is not entirely surprising when one understands the historical context within which libraries operate and realizes that librarians guided the development of these systems. The prevailing mentality behind the design of online systems was that librarians know best how to structure and retrieve information. As a result, vendors designed and developed systems in response to those ideas, but did not allow them to evolve and adapt to changing needs, even as online access and new tools for data retrieval were advancing.

## Once upon a Time

The first blinding statement of the obvious is: why do librarians not share their expertise, let go of control and create something new? The time has come for librarians to tap into new technologies and new attitudes that put the users' points of view ahead of their own. Furthermore, librarians must be vocal advocates in helping vendors develop new solutions for libraries.

By way of illustration, it might be useful to try the following experiment. Pick five libraries at random. It does not matter if the libraries are large or small, public or academic. The one thing they must have in common is a standard, integrated library system. Take, for example, the Omaha Public Library and the libraries of Howard County, Maryland; Orange County Library System in Florida; Multnomah County, Oregon; and Hennepin County, Minnesota. A search of each library's catalog to locate the DVD entitled *Once* revealed that only Hennepin County's catalog provided a fairly intuitive and relevant result. Searches in the catalogs of the other libraries required scrolling through pages of results just to find one little DVD. By comparison, Googling the word *once*—no quotation marks, just *once*—retrieved the desired item, the 2006 Irish film directed by John Carney, immediately. Searching and identifying an item by its correct title should not be this hard.

The time has come for librarians to demand and create the changes that users need. If the system vendors are not responding quickly enough, librarians should work towards developing user-friendly tools themselves. An interesting example can be found at the Robertson Library of the University of Prince Edward Island, which became the first academic library to move to the Open Source Evergreen library automation system.[1] If the Open Source concept offers viable solutions, librarians should pool their resources and collaborate with people who have the skills and knowledge to continuously adapt and improve the software so they can better serve their users and so their users can easily mine library systems for the information that they need. If librarians had relinquished control of systems and processes that they knew did not work and instead had taken bold action a decade ago, systems that provide library-centric experiences and that are built around the needs of users and are easy for users to understand would already exist. Imagine if the creators of Metacrawler or Google had grappled with the "search-all-databases-at-once" problem? The result might actually have produced a user-friendly tool that works.

Another statement of the blindingly obvious is that librarians have lost the "let a librarian help you" battle. The real issue is that the expectations librarians have created for users wishing to access library resources are simply too high, while the expectations they have created for staff performance are too low. It is a new world. Librarians must make information retrieval easier for users. The reality is that for public libraries at least a single record for all formats is what is needed, and authority control be damned! How can librarians say they are in the information business if they make information so hard to find? If librarians are serious about providing the community with the services they want, they must engage their users and seize opportunities to develop solutions that make using collections and services easier.

On December 13, 2006, *Time* recognized "You" as the Person of the Year, citing an emphasis on collaboration and community. The explosion of interest in Wikipedia and YouTube was given as the reason for the choice. In the fifteen years since the Web began to dominate our activities, a few libraries have created MySpace pages and FaceBook profiles and even a few YouTube videos, but most libraries have remained on the periphery, merely dabbing their toes into the water, rather than jumping in with a splash. Why have more libraries not engaged with their customers? Is it because they do not have the tools, the will, or the desire to do more than make a paltry attempt to nibble around the edges of interactivity? To thrive, librarians need to be bolder and to commit the staff and resources necessary so that they can take full advantage of the Internet's amazing capabilities. Perhaps librarians believe they cannot reorganize quickly enough to take advantage of all the Internet has to offer? Surely even the most resource-strapped libraries can create a think-tank or innovation team that can begin to address the challenges that face libraries and establish the stronger connections their customers require.

Several years ago many libraries began to embrace the idea of the library of the future. It may be an oversimplification to suggest that the key outcomes of that concept have been self-service and allowing food in the library, but sadly, it seems that the library's vision of the future has centered around these two areas rather than around integrating merchandizing with improvements in customer service. The library of the future requires strong, tight, mutually beneficial relationships with its customers to ensure that the customers become the library's best advocates. A broad spectrum of access, both physical and virtual, must be provided. More institutions, such as the Julia Rogers Library of Goucher College, which maintains 24/7 service during academic terms, need to operate their libraries for the convenience of their users, not for themselves.[2]

## DESIGN IS EVERYTHING

Instead of restraining their entrepreneurial impulses, librarians should follow the advice of Robert Hoekeman Jr., author of *Designing the Obvious* and founder of Miskeeto, and develop their online presence for user accessibility and ease of use.[3] It seems that many librarians are guilty of letting other people tell them what constitutes good design, which gets them bad design. They, in turn, end up forcing that bad design on their customers. Instead, librarians should make their own decisions about design and implement what they believe will work in their particular setting. For example, the principles of navigation that make it easy to find one's way around a Target store or a Costco should be incorporated into library buildings, way-finding tools, and the library's online presence.

In 2004, the Vancouver Art Gallery mounted an exhibit by designer and change agent Bruce Mau called "Massive Change: The Future of Global Design."[4] The intent of the exhibit was to see how design can be used as a methodology to address the problems inherent in society's social, economic, and political systems. Librarians can learn from ideas that come from other fields and use them as tools as they think about their collective mission for the future and about the library as place, both virtual and physical. Mau is also the author of *An Incomplete Manifesto for Growth* which identifies forty-three points that set the design world on its ear and exemplify his beliefs and his approach to all of his design projects.[5] The manifesto (figure 1) could or should have been written by and for librarians and can inform how we think about risk, change, and the future.

## WHAT IS THE BUSINESS OF LIBRARIES AND WHAT IS THE LIBRARY BRAND?

The world has a wonderful way of creating synchronicity. For example, on an episode of the CNBC television show *The Big Idea*, Richard Tait, creator of the game *Cranium,* talked about the genesis of the game and the important lessons he learned about marketing.[6] While he and his partner were lamenting that they had not introduced their game at Toy Fair—the annual toy exhibition—they realized that a more effective marketing strategy might be to market the game directly to consumers rather than through

1. **Allow events to change you.** You have to be willing to grow. Growth is different from something that happens to you. You produce it. You live it. The prerequisites for growth: the openness to experience events and the willingness to be changed by them.

2. **Forget about good.** Good is a known quantity. Good is what we all agree on. Growth is not necessarily good. Growth is an exploration of unlit recesses that may or may not yield to our research. As long as you stick to good you'll never have real growth.

3. **Process is more important than outcome.** When the outcome drives the process we will only ever go to where we've already been. If process drives outcome we may not know where we're going, but we will know we want to be there.

4. **Love your experiments (as you would an ugly child).** Joy is the engine of growth. Exploit the liberty in casting your work as beautiful experiments, iterations, attempts, trials, and errors. Take the long view and allow yourself the fun of failure every day.

5. **Go deep.** The deeper you go the more likely you will discover something of value.

6. **Capture accidents.** The wrong answer is the right answer in search of a different question. Collect wrong answers as part of the process. Ask different questions.

7. **Study.** A studio is a place of study. Use the necessity of production as an excuse to study. Everyone will benefit.

8. **Drift.** Allow yourself to wander aimlessly. Explore adjacencies. Lack judgment. Postpone criticism.

9. **Begin anywhere.** John Cage tells us that not knowing where to begin is a common form of paralysis. His advice: begin anywhere.

10. **Everyone is a leader.** Growth happens. Whenever it does, allow it to emerge. Learn to follow when it makes sense. Let anyone lead.

11. **Harvest ideas.** Edit applications. Ideas need a dynamic, fluid, generous environment to sustain life. Applications, on the other hand, benefit from critical rigor. Produce a high ratio of ideas to applications.

12. **Keep moving.** The market and its operations have a tendency to reinforce success. Resist it. Allow failure and migration to be part of your practice.

13. **Slow down.** Desynchronize from standard time frames and surprising opportunities may present themselves.

14. **Don't be cool.** Cool is conservative fear dressed in black. Free yourself from limits of this sort.

15. **Ask stupid questions.** Growth is fueled by desire and innocence. Assess the answer, not the question. Imagine learning throughout your life at the rate of an infant.

FIGURE 1   An Incomplete Manifesto for Growth by Bruce Mau

16. **Collaborate.** The space between people working together is filled with conflict, friction, strife, exhilaration, delight, and vast creative potential.

17. _____. Intentionally left blank. Allow space for the ideas you haven't had yet, and for the ideas of others.

18. **Stay up late.** Strange things happen when you've gone too far, been up too long, worked too hard, and you're separated from the rest of the world.

19. **Work the metaphor.** Every object has the capacity to stand for something other than what is apparent. Work on what it stands for.

20. **Be careful to take risks.** Time is genetic. Today is the child of yesterday and the parent of tomorrow. The work you produce today will create your future.

21. **Repeat yourself.** If you like it, do it again. If you don't like it, do it again.

22. **Make your own tools.** Hybridize your tools in order to build unique things. Even simple tools that are your own can yield entirely new avenues of exploration. Remember, tools amplify our capacities, so even a small tool can make a big difference.

23. **Stand on someone's shoulders.** You can travel farther carried on the accomplishments of those who came before you. And the view is so much better.

24. **Avoid software.** The problem with software is that everyone has it.

25. **Don't clean your desk.** You might find something in the morning that you can't see tonight.

26. **Don't enter awards competitions.** Just don't. It's not good for you.

27. **Read only left-hand pages.** Marshall McLuhan did this. By decreasing the amount of information, we leave room for what he called our _noodle_.

28. **Make new words.** Expand the lexicon. The new conditions demand a new way of thinking. The thinking demands new forms of expression. The expression generates new conditions.

29. **Think with your mind.** Forget technology. Creativity is not device-dependent.

30. **Organization = Liberty.** Real innovation in design, or any other field, happens in context. That context is usually some form of cooperatively managed enterprise. Frank Gehry, for instance, is only able to realize Bilbao because his studio can deliver it on budget. The myth of a split between creatives and suits is what Leonard Cohen calls a "charming artifact of the past."

31. **Don't borrow money.** Once again, Frank Gehry's advice. By maintaining financial control, we maintain creative control. It's not exactly rocket science, but it's surprising how hard it is to maintain this discipline, and how many have failed.

32. **Listen carefully.** Every collaborator who enters our orbit brings with him or her a world more strange and complex than any we could ever hope to imagine. By listening to the details and the subtlety of their needs, desires, or ambitions, we fold their world onto our own. Neither party will ever be the same.

(cont.)

FIGURE 1   An Incomplete Manifesto for Growth by Bruce Mau (cont.)

33. **Take field trips.** The bandwidth of the world is greater than that of your television or the Internet, or even a totally immersive, interactive, dynamically rendered, object-oriented, real-time, computer graphic–simulated environment.

34. **Make mistakes faster.** This isn't my idea—I borrowed it. I think it belongs to Andy Grove.

35. **Imitate.** Don't be shy about it. Try to get as close as you can. You'll never get all the way, and the separation might be truly remarkable. We have only to look to Richard Hamilton and his version of Marcel Duchamp's large glass to see how rich, discredited, and underused imitation is as a technique.

36. **Scat.** When you forget the words, do what Ella did: make up something else . . . but not words.

37. **Break it, stretch it, bend it, crush it, crack it, fold it.**

38. **Explore the other edge.** Great liberty exists when we avoid trying to run with the technological pack. We can't find the leading edge because it's trampled underfoot. Try using old-tech equipment made obsolete by an economic cycle but still rich with potential.

39. **Coffee breaks, cab rides, green rooms.** Real growth often happens outside of where we intend it to, in the interstitial spaces—what Dr. Seuss calls *the waiting place*. Hans Ulrich Obrist once organized a science and art conference with all of the infrastructure of a conference—the parties, chats, lunches, airport

the auspices of middlemen. Consequently, they made the game available at Starbucks and Barnes & Noble, as well as through Amazon.com, and sold a million copies of the game. Their premise was simple: take the game directly to the customers. From this experience, Tait and his partner realized that *Cranium* was not in the toy business but in the togetherness business. As librarians think about their primary business, it is worth keeping this model in mind. While they may consider themselves to be in the information business, if they are going to thrive, libraries need to expand that view to include the curiosity business, the togetherness business, the community-building business, the social networking business, and the user-centered business.

As librarians risk rocking their boats so that they can rock their users' worlds, they also have to consider their brand. While it is true that every library might have an individual brand that is unique to its user community, there is also a bigger library brand, and much more needs to be done in terms of cross-promotion and co-branding in order to change peoples' perceptions about the library. The world is increasingly mobile and a user's experience in Seattle will impact his or her perceptions about what to arrivals—but with no actual conference. Apparently it was hugely successful and spawned many ongoing collaborations.

40. **Avoid fields.** Jump fences. Disciplinary boundaries and regulatory regimes are attempts to control the wilding of creative life. They are often understandable efforts to order what are manifold, complex, evolutionary processes. Our job is to jump the fences and cross the fields.

41. **Laugh.** People visiting the studio often comment on how much we laugh. Since I've become aware of this, I use it as a barometer of how comfortably we are expressing ourselves.

42. **Remember.** Growth is only possible as a product of history. Without memory, innovation is merely novelty. History gives growth a direction. But a memory is never perfect. Every memory is a degraded or composite image of a previous moment or event. That's what makes us aware of its quality as a past and not a present. It means that every memory is new, a partial construct different from its source, and, as such, a potential for growth itself.

43. **Power to the people.** Play can only happen when people feel they have control over their lives. We can't be free agents if we're not free.

Used with permission of Bruce Mau Design (www.brucemaudesign.com). *An Incomplete Manifesto for Growth* by Bruce Mau is licensed under a Creative Commons Attribution-Noncommercial-Share Alike 3.0 Unported License.

expect in Omaha. When a public library in one location fails to meet user expectations, that perception of poor or subpar service may be ascribed to all public libraries. The same is true for experiences gained at school libraries and academic libraries. Users may have trouble differentiating between types of libraries, and librarians have not done a good job of clarifying those differences or envisioning library services and collections from the user's perspective. Instead of seeing themselves as unique, perhaps librarians need to consider what their organizations have in common and build on that commonality.

In 2007 the Wyoming State Library took a risk and created a brand that caused ripples throughout the library world.[7] Recognizing the need to bring the world to library users and to get them thinking beyond shushing librarians and musty books, the campaign included familiar images presented in new ways such as the Eiffel Tower superimposed on a Wyoming windmill, and a "mud flap girl" bumper sticker used to promote automotive databases. Clearly, the idea was to create a new image for the library, one that is risky, timely, and portrays the library as an exciting, hip place to visit. Whether one loves or hates what the Wyoming State Library did, their campaign created a buzz. The program may actually have converted some non-library users into library users, quite possibly strengthening the brand for all libraries. And the librarians at the Wyoming State Library demonstrated that it is definitely all right to publicly display a sense of humor.

## PARTNERSHIPS AND COLLABORATION EXTEND OUR REACH

Librarians are natural collaborators. Think about *Poole's Index,* or the creation of OCLC or WLN or other extraordinary efforts at building something for the collective good. Libraries must develop creative partnerships with other institutions in order to extend their reach, tap into new markets, and benefit their customers. The strategy at Omaha Public Library (OPL), a modestly funded library serving a mid-sized urban/suburban community, has been to seek out partnerships that increase the library's visibility, surprise users, and meet new demands. In recent years OPL has:

- partnered with the Henry Doorly Zoo to obtain a grant from the National Endowment for the Arts to celebrate The Big Read, the first grant in the nation awarded to a zoo and a public library;
- worked with the local National Public Radio station to sponsor a month-long visit by the StoryCorps;
- collaborated with area high schools and the Bemis Center for Contemporary Arts on an "Art 4 Omaha" project to develop public art projects for library branches;
- set up annual flu shot clinics in all library locations.[8]

These partnerships have exceeded the library's expectations and brought new users and new energy into the library. In addition, they have created new opportunities to market library services.

## THAT OF WHICH WE DARE NOT SPEAK

Even if librarians acknowledge their reluctance to change, their codependence on vendors that put profit before innovation and the reality that society is developing an assumption that libraries are no longer relevant, these issues pale in comparison to the blind spot that many librarians have regarding staff who stand in the way of change, risk-taking, and innovation.

The answer to the old joke "How many therapists does it take to change a light bulb?" ("the light bulb really has to want to change") could be rephrased for librarians as, "If we talk about it enough, we'll be able to retire and someone else can change it." Librarians really must want to change. In order to introduce change, library administrators must confront staff who appear to be unwilling or unable to change. Miriam Pollack's excellent article in *American Libraries*, "Cruel to Be Kind," discusses the need for managers to deal with problem staff instead of glossing over the problems or passing them on to others.[9] Creating expectations, documenting behavior, disciplining, demoting, reassigning, and even terminating employees can be a very painful experience. Library administrators are sometimes reluctant to take these actions, yet issues of poor performance must be addressed boldly, otherwise the dream of building the library organization of the future will be dashed. Pollack's article provides sound suggestions for building capacity within the library organization.

Within every organization there are employees who are not interested in change, innovation, or risk, who may be entrenched in their own world and have failed to change with the times, or worse, who may even work quietly and passive-aggressively to sabotage the work of those who support and implement change. Yet, due to permanent appointments, institutional culture, or simply because dealing with personnel issues is time-consuming and not something library managers are trained to do, these individuals are not often terminated. If these people cannot be persuaded to change their behavior or their attitude, library administrators need clear, documented expectations for competency and performance, and must do all they can to see that these staff members are given the opportunity to succeed, or at the very least are given assignments where they can do the least possible harm to the organization. Administrators must simultaneously pave the way for those who are motivated to teach, do outreach, explore ideas, market library services and connect with the community to do so. When opportunities to hire new staff arise, they should be hired for their flexibility, creativity, and energy in addition to other traditional qualifications. A love of books and other library materials is an insufficient qualification for interacting with the public. Unless a librarian has a desire to fully understand customer needs, he should not be working with the public. It is insensitive to the communities librarians serve, to their customers, and their organizations, to believe that staff who would rather not work with the public can ever be trained to be passionate, engaged, risk takers.

During an appearance in Omaha in 2007, author Anne Lamott said "The opposite of faith is not doubt. It is certainty."[10] Librarians need to be careful about expressing that point of view. They are often so utterly certain that the procedures they have developed are right that they are unwilling or unable to visualize an environment with happier, more satisfied users. In a world where the catch phrase is "I buy my books and I have the Internet," librarians need to be bold and liberate staff who dare to be creative and who want to develop new and better services to meet the information needs of future generations. Library leaders have a responsibility to try to get everyone on the train before it leaves the station, because, to quote the title of a book by Howard Zinn, "you can't be neutral on a moving train."[11] Those who don't wish to come along for the ride need to be where they can do the least harm.

Taking risks means that it is all right to fail and, when necessary, apologize for the failure. Librarians need the freedom to make mistakes and to learn from them. Library administrators need to foster a culture where making mistakes is acknowledged and even celebrated, not punished. Librarians need to be willing to experiment with new services and new ideas and discard those that do not work without fear of reprisals. Librarians need to be where their users are and cheer and support one another as they figure out exactly what a twenty-first-century library needs to be.

## REFERENCE NOTES

1. Marshall Breeding and Tom Peters, "Going Evergreen in Academia," *Smart Libraries Newsletter,* (July 2008), www.techsource.ala.org/sln/july-2008.html (accessed 3 February 2009). The library's home page says "Welcome to the UPEI Library Catalogue! We're proud to be the world's first academic library running Evergreen." http://island pines.roblib.upei.ca/opac/en-US/skin/roblib/xml/index.xml?ol=UPEI (accessed 8 February 2009).

2. Julia Rogers Library, Goucher College, www.goucher.edu/x643.xml (accessed 12 January 2009).

3. Robert Hoekman, *Designing the Obvious: A Common Sense Approach to Web Application Design* (Berkeley, Calif.: New Riders Pr., 2007); Miskeeto: User experience design, strategy, development, training, and more from a socially conscious collective of industry experts, http:/miskeeto.com (accessed 12 January 2009).

4. Bruce Mau, *Massive Change: The Future of Global Design,* www.vanartgallery.bc.ca/press_releases/pdf/MCpress.pdf (accessed 12 January 2009) and www.brucemaudesign.com/work_massive_change.html (accessed 12 January 2009).

5. Bruce Mau, *An Incomplete Manifesto for Growth,* www.brucemaudesign.com/manifesto.html (accessed 12 January 2009).

6. "Cranium: Have Fun, Make Millions," *The Big Idea,* www.cnbc.com/id/26642505/ (accessed 12 January 2009) and Cranium, www.hasbro.com/games/cranium/home.cfm (accessed 12 January 2009).

7. Wyoming State Library, The Wyoming Libraries Campaign, www.wyominglibraries .org/campaign.html (accessed 9 February 2009). The Wyoming State Library won the John Cotton Dana Award for this campaign in 2007.

8. The Big Read, National Endowment for the Arts, www.neabigread.org/ (accessed 5 February 2009); StoryCorps, www.storycorps.net/ (accessed 5 February 2009);

Art|4 Omaha: A Bemis Center for Contemporary Arts, Public Arts Initiative, www
.art4omaha.org/team.html (accessed 5 February 2009).

9. Miriam Pollack, "Cruel to Be Kind: Why Do We Keep Unproductive Employees?" *American Libraries* 39, no.9 (October 2008): 48.

10. Statement made by Anne Lamott and recorded by the author.

11. Howard Zinn, *You Can't Be Neutral on a Moving Train: A Personal History of Our
Times* (Boston: Beacon Pr. 1994).

# Contributors

**Marshall Keys** is an entrepreneur who has created change as a librarian, a consultant, an academic administrator, and a not-for-profit CEO. He is a member of a family of entrepreneurs whose wife, daughter, and son have created successful new ventures. He taught Information Entrepreneurship for five years at Simmons College GSLIS.

**Michael W. Carroll** is Director, Program on Information Justice and Intellectual Property at American University, Washington College of Law, Washington, D.C.

**Joyce L. Ogburn** is University Librarian and Director, J. Willard Marriott Library, University of Utah.

**Regina Reynolds** is ISSN Coordinator, Library of Congress.

**Diane Boehr** is Head of Cataloging, National Library of Medicine.

**Amy Badertscher** is Director of Collection Services, Kenyon College.

**Lynn Scott Cochrane** is Director of Libraries, Denison University.

**Jeffrey G. Trzeciak** is University Librarian, McMaster University Libraries.

**Rivkah Sass** is Executive Director, Omaha Public Library.

**Pamela Bluh** is Associate Director for Technical Services & Administration, Thurgood Marshall Law Library, University of Maryland School of Law.

**Cindy Hepfer** is Continuing Resources Cataloging Team Leader, Central Technical Services, University at Buffalo (SUNY).

CPSIA information can be obtained
at www.ICGtesting.com
Printed in the USA
FFHW020006170119
50182307-55117FF

9 780838 985168